An Atlas of Victorian Mortality

Robert Woods & Nicola Shelton

LIVERPOOL UNIVERSITY PRESS • 1997

First published 1997 by
LIVERPOOL UNIVERSITY PRESS
Senate House, Abercromby Square
Liverpool, L69 3BX

British Library Cataloguing-in-Publication Data
A British Library CIP record is available

0-85323-532-5 cased
0-85323-542-2 paper

Printed and bound in the European Union by
The Alden Press in the City of Oxford

Contents

List of Maps

List of Figures

9

List of Tables

Preface

An atlas is rather like an opera: while the maps are the highlights, there also needs to be a good text and lots of illustrations to set the scenes, but it will ultimately be judged by the impact its cartography has on the audience. Are the maps memorable? We have designed this atlas so that it can be used in a variety of ways. First, it provides a record of the data published in the Registrars General *Decennial Supplements* especially for the 1860s to the 1890s. It shows variations among the registration districts of age- and cause-specific mortality rates. The atlas is organised in terms of age groups—infancy, childhood, early adulthood and old age—and then by the principal causes of death. Separate chapters are devoted to tuberculosis, maternal mortality and violent deaths. It is introduced by four general chapters which describe the geographical units employed in the atlas, the various cause of death classifications used in the *Decennial Supplements,* the pattern of mortality variation in Victorian England and Wales and the quality of death registration. The atlas is concluded by chapters on gender variations in mortality and a short summary account which draws together the themes of 'places and diseases'.

Secondly, as well as providing a description, the atlas also considers certain issues which have been the subject of debate by demographers, medical and economic historians, and epidemiologists. The most important of these issues relate to the European mortality transition, the impact of urban growth and urbanisation, and the changing nature of (for example, scarlet fever and pulmonary tuberculosis), and possible interaction between, certain diseases (for example, measles and whooping cough). The data published in the *Decennial Supplements* for Victorian England and Wales provide perhaps the only opportunity to consider these issues in a way that takes full account of geographical variations and applies to a highly industrialised country at least half the population of which lived in urban places by 1851 and about a quarter did so even in 1801. Of course, we do not claim that we have solved any of these problems, indeed we have probably made matters appear more complicated, but we hope that our atlas will add to the various debates and perhaps even encourage new questions. We are certainly aware that there are many loose ends especially in terms of our consideration of pulmonary tuberculosis in Chapter 8 and gendered mortality differentials in Chapter 12. Also, it has not been possible to tackle the vexed question of occupational and social class mortality patterns and how they may interact via social segregation with the geographical variations which are our principal concern.

We have attempted to make the atlas as 'user friendly' as possible by our choice of colour shading and the provision of pull-out location maps (Maps A, B and C).

Appendices 1 and 2 provide, respectively, a checklist of the Registrars General *Annual Reports* and their *Decennial Supplements*, and some brief notes on the contents of the *Reports* especially as they relate to their use in this atlas. We have also adopted the convention of referring to the cause of death categories reported in the standard nosologies (Tables 2 and 5) by using an initial capital letter: Diarrhoea & Dysentery, Measles, Phthisis, Diseases of the Lung, Other causes, for example.

Grants from the Economic and Social Research Council of Great Britain (R-000-23-3373 and R-000-23-4824) for the creation of a cause of death database, and a grant towards publication costs from the Humanities Research Board of the British Academy made the preparation of the atlas possible. For this financial support, we are especially grateful. We would also like to thank the following for their assistance, helpful comments and general support: Michael Anderson, Robin Bloxsidge (of Liverpool University Press), Mark Edwards and Dave Jones (of Alden Press), Chris Galley, Bill Gould, Peter Haggett, Julie Holbrook, Gerry Kearns, Dick Lawton (for Map 34), Paul Laxton, John Marsden, Sandra Mather, Graham Mooney, Ian Qualtrough, Steve Reddy, Naomi Williams, Paul Williamson and Suzanne Yee. Our special thanks go to Alison, Rachel, Gavin and Matt who kept us going.

Department of Geography, University of Liverpool   March 1997

1
Districts

All atlases are not only expressions of geographical variation, they are also victims of the haphazard history of past administrations. This atlas is no exception. The civil registration of births, marriages and deaths began in England and Wales in 1837. Although the ecclesiastical registration of baptisms, marriages and burials continued, the new State system put in place a local framework for the certification of each individual vital event together with a centralised national administration for the collation of those certificates and the reporting of trends and variations in the vital statistics derived therefrom. The first Registrars General were either colonial civil servants or retired army officers, but they were assisted by a sequence of Compilers of Statistics or Statistical Superintendents of great eminence including perhaps the best known Victorian medical statistician, William Farr. Farr and his successors—William Ogle, John Tatham and T. H. C. Stevenson— sought not only to improve the quality of registration along with that of the decennial population censuses, but also to extend the range of material collected and its detail. Each of the Compilers was medically qualified and most had been local Medical Officers of Health before joining the General Register Office in London. The focus of their attention was therefore directed very much towards mortality statistics, public health, sanitation and thus geographical variations in the quality of especially the urban environment. The combination of these preoccupations served to create arguably the most detailed set of mortality statistics disaggregated geographically, by age, by cause of death, and often by gender, for any European country in the second half of the nineteenth century.[1]

The units used to assemble and report civil registration statistics in England and Wales between 1837 and 1910 were as follows in ascending size: registration sub-districts, registration districts, registration counties and registration divisions. Between 1837 and 1874 Registrars in the sub-districts and Superintendent Registrars in the districts were made responsible for recording birth, death and marriage events, but after 1874 the onus of responsibility was placed on parents, close relatives or the bride and groom themselves to ensure that the registration had taken place within the statutory period. Of these four levels of geographical units the smallest and therefore most numerous sub-districts would

---

[1] Muriel Nissel, *People Count: A History of the General Register Office* (London: HMSO, 1987), Simon Szreter (ed.), *The General Register Office of England and Wales and the Public Health Movement, 1837-1914, A Comparative Perspective, Social History of Medicine*, Special Issue, 4 (3) (1991), pp. 401-537, Edward Higgs, 'A cuckoo in the nest? The origins of civil registration and state medical statistics in England and Wales', *Continuity and Change* 11 (1996), pp. 115-134 and 'The statistical Big Bang of 1911: ideology, technological innovation and the production of medical statistics', *Social History of Medicine* 9 (1996), pp. 409-426, and John M. Eyler, *Victorian Social Medicine: The Ideas and Methods of William Farr* (Baltimore: Johns Hopkins University Press, 1979) provide invaluable introductions to the work of the GRO, London.

obviously provide the most detailed picture of mortality variations, but these areas were never used to report either age at death statistics or the age structure of their populations in censuses. Unfortunately, only crude birth and death rates can be calculated for sub-districts, but for the 600 or so registration districts a wide range of age-related measures may be calculated including abridged life tables for some years. Of course, an even wider range is possible for the 45 registration counties (including London and three in Wales, see Map B), the 8 divisions and England and Wales as a whole, but the districts represent the optimum geographical units with which to analyse age-standardised rates in some detail. Whilst not perfect, districts are at least superior to counties and divisions if one's objective is to capture local rather than very broad regional variations since, as contemporaries repeatedly remarked, the locality was of particular importance in the disease environment of Victorian England and Wales.

Map 1 shows the outlines of the districts used in this atlas. There are 614 units in all, with 25 for the London division (Maps 1 and C) which has to be drawn separately. Several of these districts are not original, they have been created by us by combining contemporary districts in order to permit comparison over six decades. In some cases it has also been necessary to estimate the relevant statistics using those for surrounding districts. These are not particularly serious problems for most areas of England and Wales apart from the West Riding of Yorkshire, especially the Leeds-Bradford area, and the London division. It must be noted that the 614 units do not represent a perfect solution, fewer and larger units would be required to preserve complete integrity. Rather the 614 represent a compromise solution in which every effort has been made to maximise the number of comparable units.

Map 1 was created from the original maps published to accompany the census reports, but the boundaries of the districts have been simplified to assist reproduction in atlas form where one, two or four maps of the entire set of districts will appear on a page. The broad geometry has been preserved in order to enhance visual impact and comparability, although this has meant the sacrifice of some boundary detail.[2]

It should be appreciated that the 614 districts vary in size both in terms of area and population, and that the latter also changed during the sixty years with which we are concerned. Table 1 gives some basic descriptive statistics for the population sizes of the 614 districts in 1861, 1891 and 1911. Clearly, as the size of the population of England and Wales increased from 20 millions in 1861 to 36 millions in 1911 not all districts shared in that growth. Figure 1 illustrates the point more sharply. It shows the sizes of district populations in 1861 and 1911 against the rank of those sizes from 1 to 614. Most

---

[2] Richard Lawton, 'Population changes in England and Wales in the later nineteenth century: an analysis of trends by registration districts', *Transactions of the Institute of British Geographers* 44 (1968), pp. 55-74, provides an earlier solution to the problem of generating a comparable set of units based on registration districts. Map 34 is based on Lawton's Figure 6.

Map 1. The 614 districts of England and Wales, and London

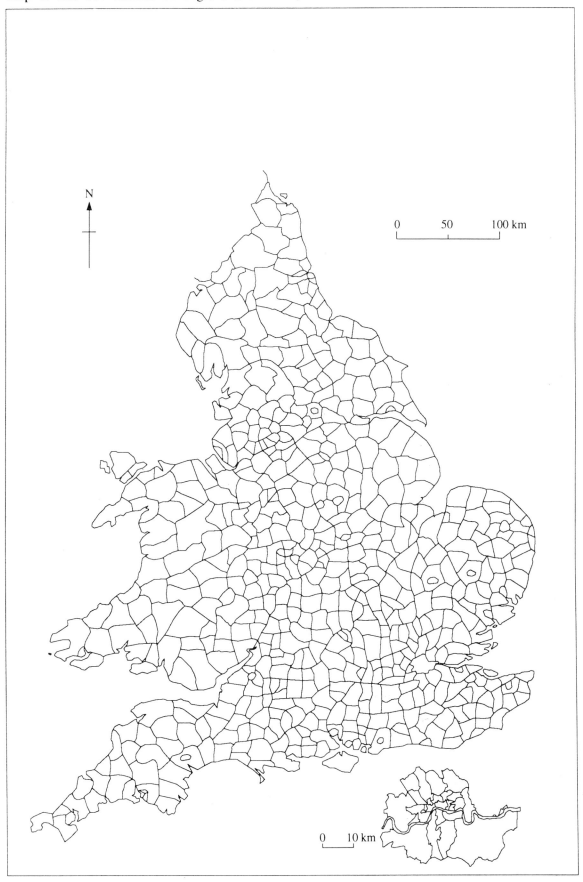

of the 16 millions increase in population occurred in the largest 50 per cent of districts. Among those districts ranked above 500 population declined so that by 1911 the frequency distribution of district population sizes was even more positively skewed than in 1861.[3] The reason for emphasising this point will become clearer in later chapters; it will be sufficient to note here that urbanisation had a profound influence on national mortality rates merely because an increasing proportion of the population became concentrated in a relatively small number of urban districts and urban districts in general tended to experience very distinctive disease environments.

This observation raises an additional problem. Some of the districts in Map 1 are truly urban, but others had a dominant urban core with surrounding rural areas (Lincoln and York are good examples). It is also true that some districts became suburbanised during the latter part of the nineteenth century, but were just beyond the urban fringe in the 1850s. It is also the case that a few districts could be said to contain only the inner city while surrounding districts housed the remainder of the urban population (Liverpool and Hull are good examples).[4] Although these are important problems, it is crucial for comparative purposes that a set of districts with fixed boundaries be defined even though such areas will be far from ideal if the intention is to describe the changing populations of distinctive built-up areas and to distinguish precisely between urban and rural places.

All the maps in this atlas were drawn using the digitised district boundaries shown in Map 1 and Arc/Info, the geographical information system. Each map has been designed to show a particular mortality index or cause of death pattern and to do so in a simple, easy to interpret and readily accessible way. The basic rates or ratios were not transformed in any sophisticated statistical fashion, therefore, and the geometry of the district boundaries was also not adjusted to allow for varying population size. Although cartograms have become a popular device for displaying spatially referenced data particularly in cases where the units are to be given equal weight (as is the case with parliamentary constituencies), or where a new image needs to be created in order to radically alter the viewer's perception of the relative importance of space (as might be the case with the world map of population distribution), in this atlas our objective is to describe simply and to encourage comparison over time, between age groups and causes. Class boundaries have been fixed on the basis of variable frequency distributions in a way that is particular to each mortality measure or cause of death, as have the colour and shading schemes. This will help to draw out the most important features of each

[3] C. M. Law, 'The growth of urban population in England and Wales, 1801-1911', *Transactions of the Institute of British Geographers* 41 (1967), pp. 125-143, and Richard Lawton, 'Urbanisation and population change in nineteenth-century England', in John Patten (ed.) *The Expanding City* (London: Academic Press, 1983), pp. 179-224, chart the changing level and pattern of urbanisation using census and registration district material.

[4] See Paul Laxton and Naomi Williams, 'Urbanization and infant mortality in England: a long term perspective and review', in Marie C. Nelson and John Rogers (eds.), *Urbanisation and the Epidemiologic Transition*, Reports from the Family History Group, Department of History, Uppsala University, No. 9 (Uppsala, 1989), pp. 109-135, especially Figure 3.

Table 1. Descriptive statistics for the distribution of population among 614 districts, England and Wales, 1861, 1891 and 1911.

	1861	1891	1911
Minimum	2497	2990	2396
Maximum	269742	572790	749395
Range	267245	569800	746999
Mean	32588	47344	58939
Median	20243	23212	24829
Standard deviation	35267	63920	86105

Source: Population Censuses of England and Wales, 1861, 1891 and 1911.

Figure 1. Distribution of 614 English and Welsh districts ranked by population size, 1861 and 1911 compared

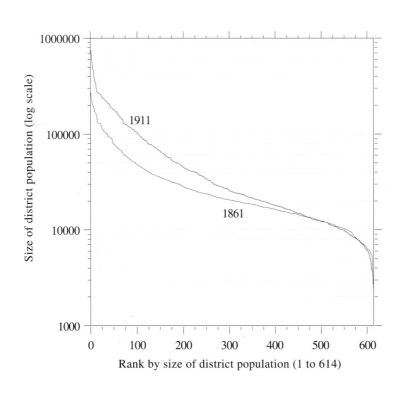

19

distribution. Although cartographic purists may disparage our *ad hoc* approach, we are convinced that this is the best way to portray variations and changes in level, age at and cause of death.[5]

[5] Other medical or epidemiological atlases have adopted different approaches. See, for example, G. Melvyn Howe, *National Atlas of Disease Mortality in the United Kingdom* (London: Thomas Nelson and Sons, 1963, second edition 1970) also *Man, Environment and Diseases in Britain* (Newton Abbot: David & Charles, 1972), pp. 184-244 especially Figures 79 and 81-90, M. J. Gardner, P. D. Winter and David J. P. Barker, *Atlas of Mortality from Selected Diseases in England and Wales, 1968-1978* (Chichester: Wiley, 1984), Andrew D. Cliff and Peter Haggett, *Atlas of Disease Distributions: Analytic Approaches to Epidemiological Data* (Oxford: Blackwell, 1988), Daniel Dorling, *A New Social Atlas of Britain* (Chichester: Wiley, 1995), Tony Champion *et al.*, *The Population of Britain in the 1990s: A Social and Economic Atlas* (Oxford: Clarendon Press, 1996).

2

Nosologies

One of the principal objectives of William Farr and his successors at the General Register Office was to chart the changing and geographically varying pattern of mortality by age, place, cause of death and occupation in Victorian England and Wales. Perhaps because of the background of the Statistical Superintendents the new civil registration system's greatest triumph became the detailed record it provided of the numbers dying and the reason for their demise.[6] From the start of registration in 1837 each Registrar General was obliged to lay before Parliament an *Annual Report* which contained statistical material and to which was attached increasingly more comprehensive statistical abstracts. Farr began the practice of writing open letters to the Registrar General and of developing both the descriptive and interpretative aspects of the *Reports* until by mid-century they had become comprehensive accounts of the country's demographic state.

Appendix 1 gives a check-list of the *Annual Reports* and their location in British Parliamentary Papers, together with the population censuses between 1851 and 1911. It highlights the fact that from the *Twenty-fifth Annual Report* the Registrar General began to provide a *Decennial Supplement* to act as a summary of vital statistics for an entire decade. It is from the six *Decennial Supplements* for the 1850s to the 1900s that we draw the material upon which this atlas is largely based although, as Appendix 2 suggests, there is much other important data to be found in the *Annual Reports* themselves.[7]

Each of the six *Decennial Supplements* reports the numbers who have died by age group, by registration district, by cause of death, although not always by gender. Elsewhere in the *Annual Reports* it is possible to consider mortality by age annually (until 1883 at least) and cause of death (but not age) for the registration districts, but only for decades and via tables in the *Supplements* may one deal with districts, ages and causes in combination. We have already considered the problem of defining consistent boundaries for comparable districts, now we must turn to the reporting of cause of death.

During the four decades he served at the General Register Office, Farr made strenuous efforts to develop simple but effective nosologies with which to describe and classify

---

[6] See John M. Eyler, 'Mortality statistics and Victorian health policy: program and criticism', *Bulletin of the History of Medicine* 50 (1976), pp. 335-355 and Sir Arthur Newsholme, *The Elements of Vital Statistics in their Bearing on Social and Public Health Problems* (London: George Allen and Unwin, first edition 1889, third edition 1923) for accounts of the uses of medical statistics, of death registration and the certification of cause of death.

[7] M. Britton (ed.), *Mortality and Geography: A Review of the Mid-1980s*, Registrar General's Decennial Supplement for England and Wales, Series DS No. 9 (London: HMSO, 1990), Table 1.1, p. 2, contains a checklist of geographically disaggregated cause by age data published by the Registrar General, 1851-1860 to 1969-1973.

causes of death. He was of course greatly handicapped by imperfect epidemiological knowledge, by local and temporal variations in the practice of death certification, by the administrative competence of district Registrars and the army of tally clerks employed to sift and sort certificates, by the sheer volume of the task and so forth. Given these difficulties it is not surprising that Victorian nosologies changed to reflect new knowledge and revised practice, and that they are far less precise than the standard international cause of death classifications that began to be applied from the early years of the twentieth century. These early nosologies are as much a reflection of Victorian confidence in science as the railways and steamships of the age.[8]

Table 2 shows the nosologies used by William Farr (1851-1860 and 1861-1870), William Ogle (1871-1880), John Tatham (1881-1890 and 1891-1900) and T. H. C. Stevenson (1901-1910) to report causes of death for the registration districts in an age-disaggregated fashion in the *Decennial Supplements*. They are clearly not the most detailed nosologies possible, but with 25 separate categories, 17 age groups, at least 600 districts and two sexes it is difficult to see how more causes could have been specified in such a summary. Table 2 has been laid out to permit comparison along the rows although this is not always a straightforward matter. The symbol • is used to denote a new category. The most radical changes in nosology came in 1901. These changes make it very difficult to compare all but a handful of the infectious diseases and for this reason 1901-1910 has for most purposes been excluded from detailed consideration here. The next most significant change to the nosology came in 1881 and was applied retrospectively by Ogle in his *Supplement* for 1871-1880. Farr had used eight broad categories under the heading *Diseases of:* by focusing on the general location in the body where the principal symptoms were to be found — brain, heart, lung, liver, kidneys, etc. The new version implemented by Ogle adopted rather more rigorous medical terms—diseases of the respiratory, circulatory, nervous systems, etc. Although an improvement in principle, the new nosology did not necessarily assist comparability nor did it affect the fundamental problem encountered in all systems of death certification: the use by those completing the original certificate of imprecise language to describe only the most immediate and obvious cause or no cause at all but a general condition ('fever', 'fright', 'fall from a horse' or 'old age', for example). By comparison 'bronchitis', 'Bright's disease' and

---

[8] See especially the *Seventh, Sixteenth, Twenty-first* and *Twenty-seventh Annual Reports* which contain letters from Farr to the Registrar General on the classification of causes of death (Appendix 1). Anne Hardy, ''Death is the cure of all diseases': using the General Register Office cause of death statistics for 1837-1920', *Social History of Medicine* 7 (1994), pp. 472-492, and Naomi Williams, 'The reporting and classification of causes of death in mid-nineteenth-century England: the example of Sheffield', *Historical Methods* 29 (1996), pp. 58-71, provide valuable introductions to the cause of death statistics themselves.

Table 2. Nosologies used in Registrars General *Decennial Supplements* to report cause of death for registration districts, England and Wales, 1851-1860 to 1901-1910

1851-1860	1861-1870	1871-1880	1881-1890	1891-1900	1901-1910
•Smallpox	•Smallpox	•Smallpox	•Smallpox	•Smallpox	•Smallpox
•Measles	•Measles	•Measles	•Measles	•Measles	•Measles
•Scarlet fever	•Scarlet fever	•Scarlet fever	•Scarlet fever	•Scarlet fever	•Scarlet fever
•Diphtheria	•Diphtheria	•Diphtheria	•Diphtheria	•Diphtheria	•Diphtheria
•Whooping cough	•Whooping cough	•Whooping cough	•Whooping cough	•Whooping cough	•Whooping cough
					•Influenza
•Typhus, Typhoid	•Typhus	•Typhus	•Typhus	•Typhus	•Typhus
•Cholera, Diarrhoea and Dysentery					
	•Cholera	•Cholera	•Cholera	•Cholera	•Cholera
	•Diarrhoea and Dysentery	•Diarrhoea and Dysentery	•Diarrhoea and Dysentery	•Diarrhoea and Dysentery	•Diarrhoea and Dysentery
		•Enteric fever	•Enteric fever	•Enteric fever	•Enteric fever
		•Simple continued fever	•Simple continued fever	•Simple continued fever	•Simple continued fever
					•Pyrexia
•Other zymotic diseases	•Other zymotic diseases				
•Cancer	•Cancer	•Cancer	•Cancer	•Cancer	•Cancer
•Scrofula and Tabes mesenterica	•Scrofula and Tabes mesenterica				
		•Scrofula			
		•Tabes mesenterica	•Tabes mesenterica	•Tabes mesenterica	•Tabes mesenterica
•Phthisis	•Phthisis	•Phthisis	•Phthisis	•Phthisis	
			•Other tuberculous and Scrofulous diseases	•Other tuberculous and Scrofulous diseases	
•Hydrocephalus	•Hydrocephalus	•Hydrocephalus			
Diseases of:	*Diseases of:*	*Diseases of:*	*Diseases of:*	*Diseases of:*	†
•Brain	•Brain	•Nervous system	•Nervous system	•Nervous system	
•Heart and Dropsy	•Heart and Dropsy	•Circulatory system	•Circulatory system	•Circulatory system	
•Lung	•Lung	•Respiratory system	•Respiratory system	•Respiratory system	
•Stomach and Liver	•Stomach and Liver	•Digestive system	•Digestive system	•Digestive system	
•Kidneys	•Kidneys	•Urinary system	•Urinary system	•Urinary system	
•Generative organs	•Generative organs	•Generative organs	•Generative organs	•Generative organs	
•Joints	•Joints				
•Skin	•Skin				
		•Puerperal fever	•Puerperal fever	•Puerperal fever	•Puerperal fever and Childbirth
•Childbirth and Metria	•Childbirth and Metria	•Childbirth	•Childbirth	•Childbirth	
	•Suicide	•Suicide			
•Violent deaths	•Other violent deaths	•Other violent deaths	•Violence	•Violence	•Violence
•Other causes	•Other causes	•Other causes	•Other causes	•Other causes	•Other causes

Notes: † The 1901-1910 classification also contains the following causes of death: •Pulmonary tuberculosis, •Phthisis (not otherwise defined), •Tuberculous meningitis, •Tuberculous peritonitis, •Other tuberculous diseases, •Septic diseases, •Rheumatic fever and Rheumatism of heart, •Pneumonia, •Bronchitis.

The 1871-1880, 1881-1890 and 1891-1900 *Supplements* do not report the causes of deaths for males and females separately.

The 1851-1860 and 1861-1870 *Supplements* report age at death in the following categories:

0, 1, 2, 3, 4, 0-4, 5-9, 10-14, 15-19, 20-24, 25-34, 35-44, 45-54, 55-64, 65-74, 75-84, and 85+. The others use 75+ and the 1901-1910 *Supplement* gives 2-4 instead of 2, 3 and 4.

Each of the six *Supplements* gives inter-census mean populations by age groups, but in 1851-1860 single years under 5 are not stated.

All but the 1851-1860 and 1861-1870 *Supplements* give the total number of births.

See Appendices 1 and 2.

'measles' would prove simple to classify.[9] Although there is a rough equivalence between Diseases of the Lung and Diseases of the Respiratory system, and between Diseases of the Brain and Diseases of the Nervous system, care must be taken not to infer an exact translation.

Probably the most secure set of causes in terms of ease of recognition and thus certification is that group of diseases to which young children—although not necessarily infants under the age of 1 year—were most vulnerable.[10] The classic infectious childhood diseases of smallpox, measles, scarlet fever, diphtheria and whooping cough were all readily distinguishable in the Victorian period and could be recognised by parents and doctors alike even though their aetiology might not be properly understood or, apart from smallpox, their incidence effectively prevented.[11] These five causes of death might be traced through six decades, but for the absence of stated 'at risk' populations under 5 years for 1851-1860. They will provide the focus for Chapter 6 on young children.

Deaths in childbirth and from puerperal fever, together with those from violent causes including suicide in the 1860s and 1870s, provides another set of causes which would appear relatively consistently reported in the various nosologies. However, as we shall see in Chapter 9 maternal mortality poses particular measurement problems and the deaths from violent causes which are considered in Chapter 11 also raise well-known issues of definition.

Of the remaining broad groups of causes of death the various forms of tuberculosis (phthisis or pulmonary tuberculosis appears consistently in the classifications); the water-borne diseases, especially cholera, diarrhoea and dysentery, typhoid or enteric fever; and cancer (a deceptively simple category) may also prove useful for certain age groups and once again, when treated with extreme caution in terms of consistency and comparability.[12]

---

[9] Henry Payne, *A Pocket Vocabulary of Medical Terms (with their pronunciation), for the use of Registrars, Poor Law Officials, &C.* (London: Hadden, Best & Co, 1885) provides interesting examples of the problems encountered. At the other extreme of the nosology spectrum see, Robert Woods, 'Physician, heal thyself: the health and mortality of Victorian doctors', *Social History of Medicine* 9 (1996), pp. 1-30, especially Table 5, pp. 12-13, for Ogle's work on a nosology for the medical profession, also Arthur Newsholme, 'The vital statistics of Peabody Buildings and other artisans' and labourers' block dwellings', *Journal of the Royal Statistical Society* 54 (1891), pp. 70-97, provide examples of very detailed classifications.

[10] The *Fifth-fourth Annual Report* for 1891 contains special tabulations on the cause of death of infants in three towns and three counties for 1889-1891 devised by William Ogle and shown here in Table 5. The classification of cause of death in infancy will be discussed at greater length in Chapters 4 and 5.

[11] See Charles West, *Lectures on the Diseases of Infancy and Childhood* (London: Longmans, Green and Co., seventh edition 1884)

[12] On the problems of tuberculosis registration in the twentieth century see, Linda Bryder, "Not always one and the same thing': the registration of tuberculosis deaths in Britain, 1900-1950', *Social History of Medicine* 9 (1996), pp. 253-265. Kenneth F. Kiple (ed.), *The Cambridge World History of Human Disease* (Cambridge: Cambridge University Press, 1993) provides the most comprehensive guide to aetiologies and their histories. And on cancer statistics, Arthur Newsholme, 'The statistics of cancer', *The Practitioner* (April 1899), pp. 371-384, who argues that 'the increase in cancer is only apparent, and is due to improved diagnosis and more careful certification of the causes of death, especially in the latter.' (p. 384) (See also footnote 77.)

Finally the category Other causes needs to be considered separately because, as well shall see in Chapter 4, the percentage of deaths lumped into this residual category varied considerably among age groups. It may thereby provide a means to offer some form of evaluation of the quality of the cause of death registration and reporting systems.

3

General mortality patterns and structures

Before we begin to develop the atlas proper it is important to establish the broad outline of mortality variations in Victorian England and Wales.[13] The most obvious starting point is the series of official full English life tables begun in the 1840s by William Farr and symbolising his hopes for nosometry, the numerical method and their application to matters of health.[14] Table 3 gives life expectancies in years for selected ages drawn from English Life Tables 3 to 9. English Life Tables 1 and 2 for 1841 and 1838-1844, respectively, have been ignored largely because the age structure data used to estimate population at risk of dying by age were drawn from only one census, 1841. During the second half of the nineteenth century life expectancy at birth improved by about 7 to 8 years. Not perhaps a dramatic shift, but one that took national life expectancy at birth to levels not previously experienced.[15] In the early twentieth century the pace of change did begin to accelerate influenced especially by the rapid decline of infant mortality.

It is well known that what mortality decline that did occur between mid-century and 1901 was focused on only a limited age range.[16] Life expectancy at age 60 and 40, even 20, improved only very slowly, but there was substantial decline among children and young adults. The partial life expectancies 1-15, 15-35 and 35-65 have been included in Table 3 to make this point. In the 1840s children in the age group 1-15 lived on average

[13] See, by way of introduction, Robert Woods, *The Population of Britain in the Nineteenth Century* (Cambridge: Cambridge University Press, 1995), Robert Woods and John Woodward (eds.), *Urban Disease and Mortality in Nineteenth-Century England* (London: Batsford, 1984), Robert Woods and P. R. Andrew Hinde, 'Mortality in Victorian England: models and patterns', *Journal of Interdisciplinary History* 18 (1987), pp. 27-54, and for rather more general accounts by medical historians, F. B. Smith, *The People's Health, 1830-1910* (London: Croom Helm, 1979) and Anthony S. Wohl, *Endangered Lives: Public Health in Victorian Britain* (London: Dent, 1983). There is still much of great value in William Farr, *Vital Statistics* (London: Sanitary Institute of Great Britain, edited by Noel Humphreys, 1885). Although this *Atlas* is clearly a product of the demographic and epidemiological tradition, there are many other potentially complementary approaches which tackle the social and psychological significance of death; these are illustrated by Pat Jalland, *Death in the Victorian Family* (Oxford: Oxford University Press, 1996).

[14] See John M. Eyler, 'The conceptual origins of William Farr's epidemiology: numerical methods and social thought in the 1830s', in Abraham M. Lilienfeld (ed.), *Times, Places, and Persons: Aspects of the History of Epidemiology* (Baltimore: Johns Hopkins University Press, 1980), pp. 1-21, and Sir Arthur Newsholme, 'The measurement of progress in public health with special reference to the life and work of William Farr', *Economica* 9 (1923), pp. 186-202.

[15] É. A. Wrigley and R. S. Schofield, *The Population History of England, 1541-1871: A Reconstruction* (London: Edward Arnold, 1981; Cambridge: Cambridge University Press, 1989) provides estimates of life expectancy at birth from the middle of the sixteenth century.

[16] Thomas McKeown and R. G. Record, 'Reasons for the decline of mortality in England and Wales during the nineteenth century', *Population Studies* 16 (1962), pp. 94-122, Thomas McKeown, R. G. Record and R. D. Turner, 'An interpretation of the decline of mortality in England and Wales during the twentieth century', *Population Studies* 29 (1975), pp. 391-422, and Thomas McKeown, *The Modern Rise of Population* (London: Edward Arnold, 1976). The 'McKeown interpretation' will be considered at greater length in Chapter 13.

Table 3. Life expectancies in years at selected ages for males and females (in italics), England and Wales, 1838-1854 to 1920-1922

Age	ELT 3 1838-1854	ELT 4 1871-1880	ELT 5 1881-1890	ELT 6 1891-1900	ELT 7 1901-1910	ELT 8 1910-1912	ELT 9 1920-1922
0	39.9	41.4	43.7	44.1	48.5	51.5	55.6
	41.9	*44.6*	*47.2*	*47.8*	*52.4*	*55.4*	*59.6*
5	49.7	50.9	52.8	53.5	55.9	57.1	58.8
	50.3	*53.1*	*54.9*	*55.8*	*58.5*	*59.9*	*61.7*
10	47.1	47.6	49.0	49.6	51.8	53.1	54.6
	47.7	*49.8*	*51.1*	*52.0*	*54.5*	*55.9*	*57.5*
20	39.5	39.4	40.3	41.0	43.0	44.2	45.8
	40.3	*41.7*	*42.4*	*43.4*	*45.8*	*47.1*	*48.7*
40	26.1	25.3	25.4	25.6	26.9	27.7	29.2
	27.3	*27.5*	*27.6*	*27.8*	*29.4*	*30.3*	*31.9*
60	12.5	13.1	12.9	12.9	13.5	13.8	14.4
	14.3	*14.2*	*14.1*	*14.1*	*15.0*	*15.5*	*16.2*
80	4.9	4.8	4.5	4.6	4.9	4.9	4.9
	5.3	*5.2*	*5.0*	*5.1*	*5.4*	*5.5*	*5.6*
1-15	3.5	4.6	6.5	7.0	8.4	8.9	10.0
	3.4	*4.5*	*6.7*	*6.9*	*8.2*	*8.9*	*9.9*
15-35	13.8	14.8	15.6	16.0	16.5	16.9	17.9
	13.3	*14.7*	*15.4*	*16.1*	*16.8*	*17.1*	*17.0*
35-65	18.6	18.1	18.6	18.9	20.0	20.7	21.9
	19.1	*19.5*	*19.9*	*20.3*	*21.3*	*22.0*	*23.2*

Source: English Life Tables 3 to 9

only 25 per cent of the maximum possible 14 years, by 1910-1912 this had risen to 64 per cent.[17] Similarly in the 1840s those aged 15-35 lived 68 per cent of the maximum time possible and this increased to 85 per cent by 1910-1912 (for those aged 35-65 the percentages are 63 and 70). National infant mortality rates did not decline before 1901, however (see Figure 12). The importance of only a limited age range in which mortality improvement occurred is demonstrated even more clearly in Figure 2. Outside the age range 1-50 very little reduction occurred in the last half of the nineteenth century, but what happened to improve the life chances of children and young adults, and thus to reduce the level of mortality in general, remains a complicated story.

[17] Partial life expectancy between two ages is given by the difference between the life expectancies at those ages in years. For example, e_{1-15} would be $e_1 - e_{15}$. It would be 14 years if no one died.

Figure 2. Age-specific mortality curves for decades,
England and Wales, 1851-1860 to 1891-1900

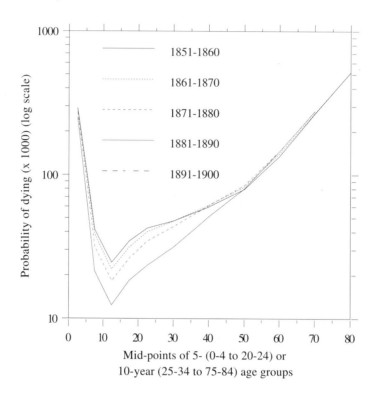

Mid-points of 5- (0-4 to 20-24) or
10-year (25-34 to 75-84) age groups

Although we are concerned in this atlas with the way in which mortality declined, and certainly with how it varied by age, our principal objective must be to illustrate how mortality varied geographically and the extent to which that variation changed between the 1850s and the 1900s. To that end Maps 2 and 3 show life expectancy at birth and at age 20 (e_0 and e_{20} in life table notation) in years for the total population in 1861-1863. Although for England and Wales as a whole at this time both e_0 and e_{20} were about 40-41 years, there were isolated districts and some larger rural areas whose populations even then enjoyed life expectancies more in keeping with national levels of the 1920s. Farr's Healthy Districts life table for 1849-1853 gives an e_0 of nearly 50 (with 53 for the 1880s and 54 for the 1890s), a level which came close to being set as an attainable standard, a Victorian mortality barometer.[18]

Conversely, there were also substantial areas with very high mortality where life chances were significantly below what was attainable in the most favoured environments. Although relatively few in number, what was important about these districts was that they were invariably urban, they formed regional clusters, they contained a very substantial

[18] William Farr, 'On the construction of life-tables; illustrated by a new life-table of the healthy districts of England', *Philosophical Transactions of the Royal Society of London* 149 (1859), pp. 837-878, reflects Farr's hope that by selecting a group of largely rural, low mortality registration districts a standard could be established against which the inadequacies and progress of public health could be measured (see Figures 29 and 44 for examples of the use of Healthy Districts Life Tables).

Map 2. Life expectancy at birth in years, 1861 – 1863

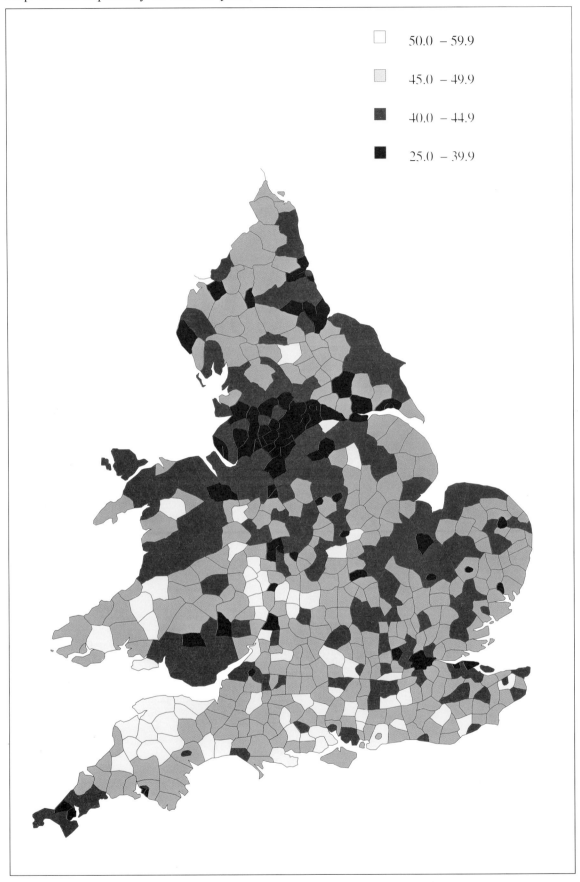

50.0 – 59.9

45.0 – 49.9

40.0 – 44.9

25.0 – 39.9

Map 3. Life expectancy at age 20 in years, 1861 – 1863

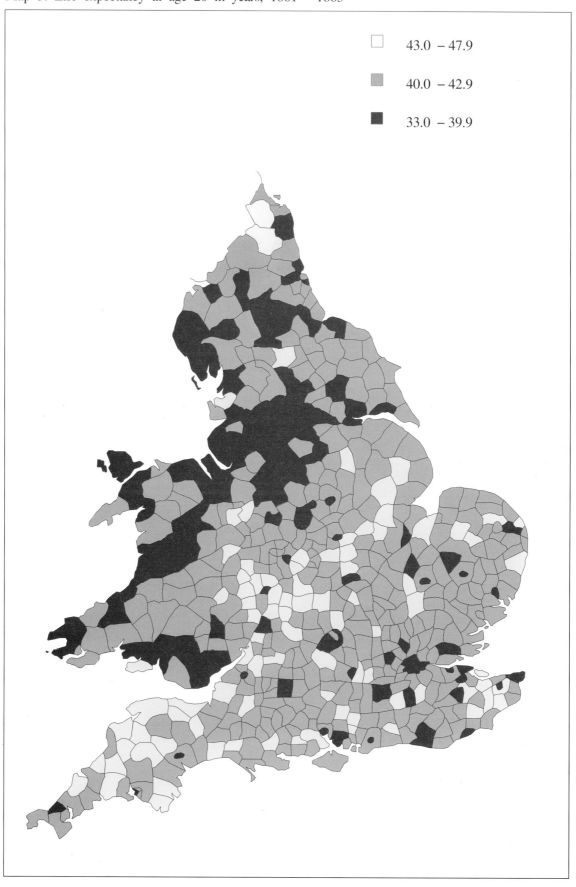

43.0 – 47.9

40.0 – 42.9

33.0 – 39.9

proportion of the English and Welsh population and, as Figure 1 illustrates, that urban proportion was increasing throughout the nineteenth century. Figure 3 uses the 614 districts and estimates of e_0 in the 1860s and 1890s to show how, although the range of mortality experience did not alter, the percentage of the English and Welsh population living in districts with given levels of life expectancy at birth shifted between the decades. In the 1860s no more than 13 per cent of the population lived in districts with an e_0 of 50 or more, by the 1890s it was about 25 per cent. Some 40 per cent lived in districts with an e_0 less than 40 in the 1860s, but about 14 per cent in the 1890s. Applying the same procedure to the infant mortality rate (IMR) and the early childhood mortality rate (ECMR, ages 1 to 4 in completed years) gives rather different impressions for, as we shall see in greater detail in Chapters 5 and 6, IMR varied considerably in geographical terms, but did not change nationally, while ECMR both varied and changed. Figures 4 and 5 make these points and will be returned to in due course.[19]

Figure 3. Percentage of the population of England and Wales living in districts with particular levels of life expectancy at birth, 1861-1870 and 1891-1900

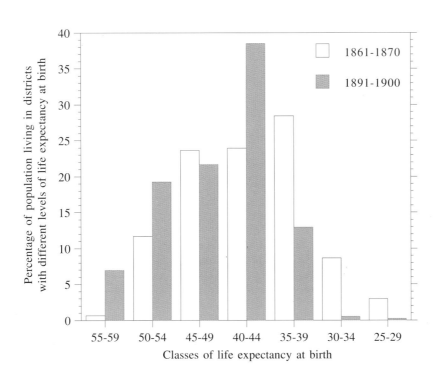

[19] Naomi Williams and Graham Mooney, 'Infant mortality in an 'Age of Great Cities': London and the English provincial cities compared, c. 1840-1910', *Continuity and Change* 9 (1994), pp. 185-212, and Naomi Williams and Chris Galley, 'Urban-rural differentials in infant mortality in Victorian England', *Population Studies* 49 (1995), pp. 401-420 illustrate these points for infant mortality.

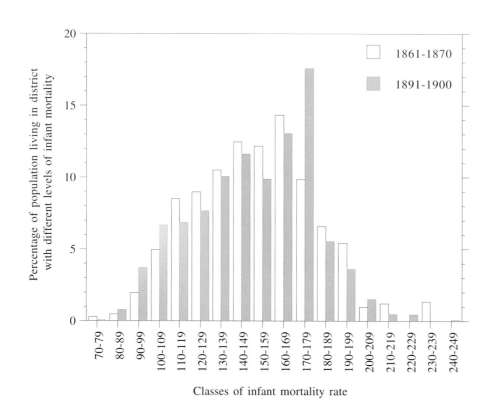

Figure 4. Percentage of the population of England and Wales living in districts with particular levels of infant mortality (IMR), 1861-1870 and 1891-1900

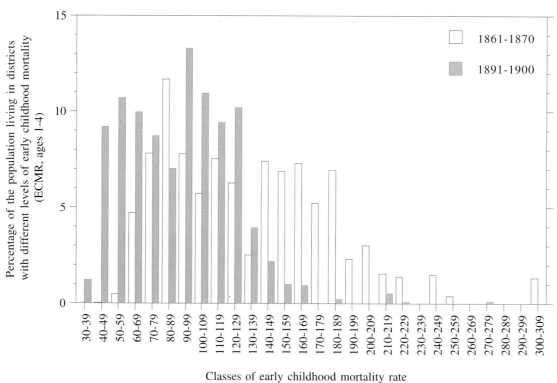

Figure 5. Percentage of the population of England and Wales living in districts with particular levels of early childhood mortality (ECMR), 1861-1870 and 1891-1900

While it is a relatively straightforward matter to demonstrate how mortality varied with age, with place and environment, how the age relationship changed, how the redistribution of population may have had a bearing on changing national mortality levels and how the proportion of the population of England and Wales experiencing particular rates of mortality shifted as a partial consequence; it becomes far more difficult when one wishes to consider age at death and cause of death distinguishing changes over time and between males and females. Such an exercise is essential, however, as a preliminary to the description of geographical variations in causes of death. Figure 6 uses data for the 1860s and the 1890s for England and Wales as a whole, the nosologies and age groups outlined in Table 2, and it distinguishes between males and females. Figure 7 repeats the exercise for London.

Figures 6 and 7 are designed to allow the comparison of males and females within each graph and decades across the rows for the same age group. They enable the most important causes of death in each age group to be identified easily.

In the nosology adopted in the *Decennial Supplements* mortality in infancy is dominated by Other causes followed by Diseases of the Brain (Nervous system) and Diseases of the Lung (Respiratory system), then Diarrhoea & Dysentery. But for early and later childhood (ages 1-4 and 5-9) the pattern changes dramatically. Now Other causes takes a far lower share of deaths and the infectious diseases of childhood—especially Scarlet fever, Measles, Whooping cough and Diphtheria—are dominant alongside Diseases of the Lung (Respiratory diseases). In later childhood Scarlet fever is especially important in the 1860s but declines by the 1890s whereas Diphtheria is more prominent in the 1890s. Measles, Whooping cough and Diphtheria also show excess mortality among girls especially in the 1890s.

Mortality, as Figure 2 shows, is at its lowest and declining for the age group 10-14 (see also Figures 28 and 29). By these ages and certainly by the 1890s, the diseases associated with childhood have given way to those of early adulthood, especially Phthisis (pulmonary tuberculosis). This becomes the dominant cause of mortality in the late teens and early twenties, and indeed well into the middle years of life. The nineteenth century was much more the age of tuberculosis than of cholera. By the forties and fifties Diseases of the Heart (Circulatory system), the Lung (Respiratory system) and the Brain (Nervous system) became more prominent alongside Cancer, and by the sixties and seventies these were the dominant causes of death, although Other causes returns to importance in extreme old age.[20]

[20] Samuel H. Preston, Nathan Keyfitz and Robert Schoen, *Causes of Death: Life Tables for National Populations* (New York: Seminar Press, 1972) and Samuel H. Preston, *Mortality Patterns in National Populations* (New York: Academic Press, 1976) develop the analysis of international variations in cause of death patterns further than is possible here.

Figure 6. Cause of death rates by age and gender, England and Wales, 1861-1870 and 1891-1900

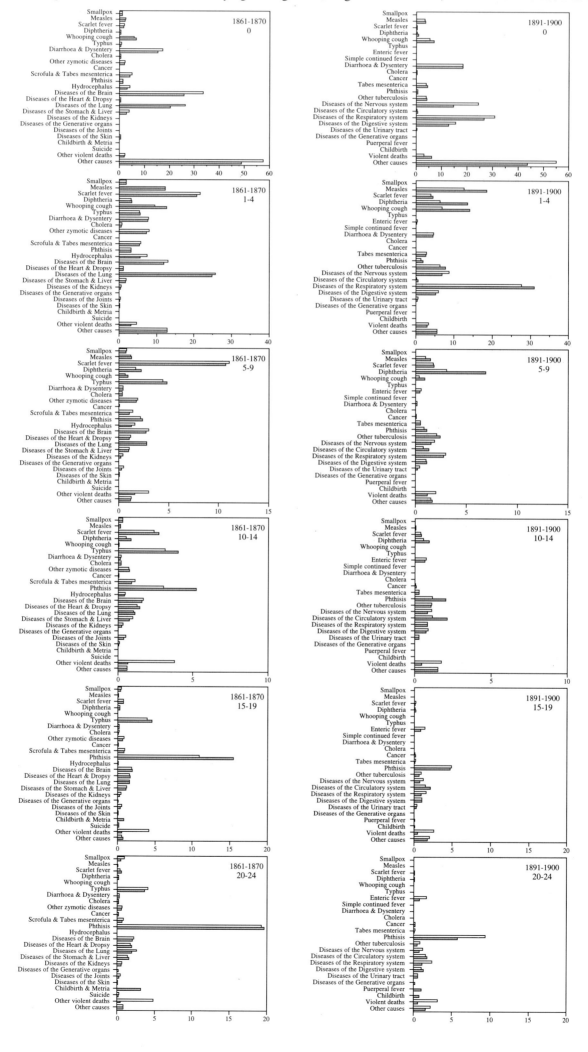

Figure 6 (continued). Cause of death rates by age and gender, England and Wales, 1861-1870 and 1891-1900

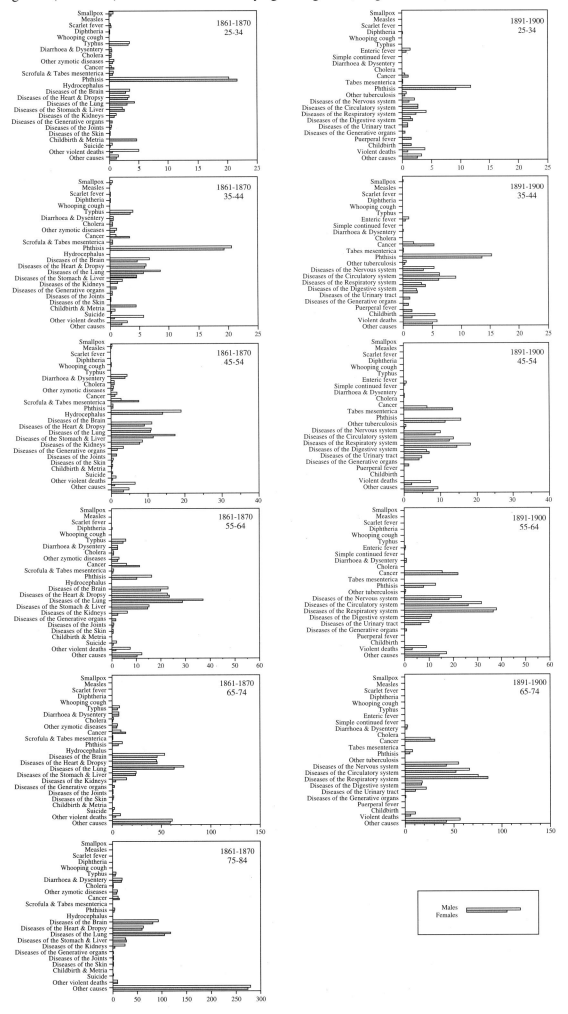

Figure 7. Cause of death rates by age and gender, London, 1861-1870 and 1891-1900

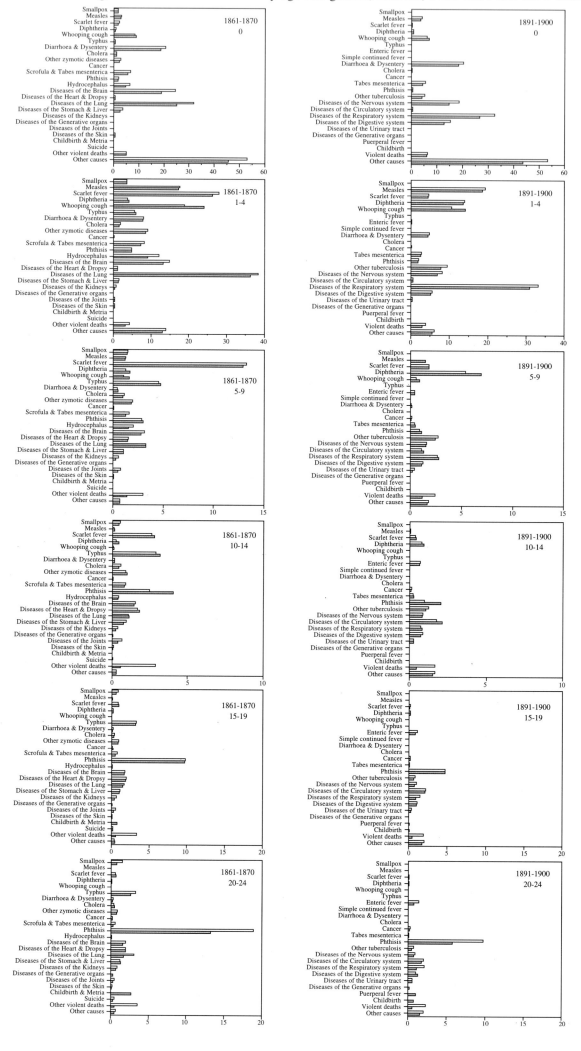

Figure 7 (continued). Cause of death rates by age and gender, London, 1861-1870 and 1891-1900

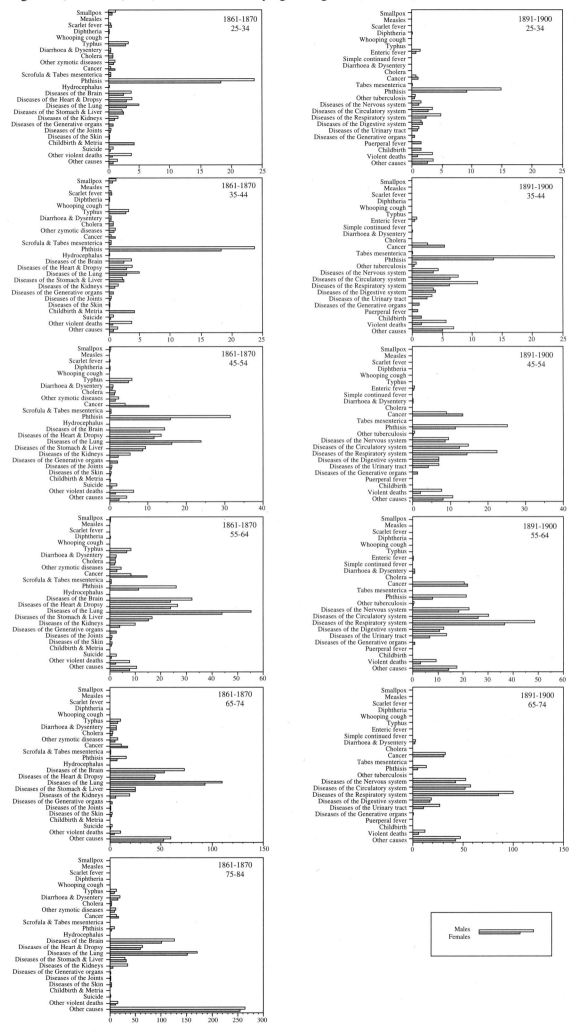

4

The quality of death registration

It must be said at the outset that it is extremely difficult, if not impossible, to provide a comprehensive evaluation of the quality of death registration in Victorian England. Earlier attempts by Glass and Teitelbaum to assess the quality of birth registration post-1837 largely assumed that the registration of deaths was relatively accurate, at least in terms of total numbers.[21] For example, Teitelbaum has concluded that, 'Except for mortality very soon after birth, it seems likely that the registration of deaths in nineteenth-century Britain was more complete than birth registration.'[22] Even if their assumption is correct, any work that deals with such additional categories as age, location, gender and cause of death must be especially sensitive to the likelihood of systematic misreporting as well as the possibility that the nature of such errors may vary from decade to decade.

The calculation of accurate age-specific mortality measures requires not only deaths by age, but also the number of those living by age. The former comes from death certification and could in principle be cross-checked with birth certification, while the latter is regularly recorded in population censuses (at least since 1841). In both cases age-heaping because of misreporting is likely. Systematic age-recording errors in both the numerators and denominators of the data used to calculate mortality rates were well known to nineteenth-century actuaries. Farr's work on the first three official English Life Tables was largely concerned with the misreporting of age and the application of methods designed to smooth away the resulting systematic errors. In the case of these full life tables, ages are recorded in single years whereas age data in the *Decennial Supplements* can appear in single, five-year or ten-year groupings. Therefore, it is not only difficult to detect under-registration of deaths, but also the misreporting of age at death.[23]

[21] D. V. Glass, 'A note on the under-registration of births in Britain in the nineteenth century', *Population Studies* 5 (1951), pp. 70-88, Michael S. Teitelbaum, 'Birth underregistration in the constituent counties of England and Wales: 1841-1910', *Population Studies* 28 (1974), pp. 329-343. See also W. P. D. Logan, 'Mortality in England and Wales from 1848 to 1947. A survey of the changing causes of death during the past hundred years', *Population Studies* 4 (1950), pp. 132-178.

[22] Michael S. Teitelbaum, *The British Fertility Decline: Demographic Transition in the Crucible of the Industrial Revolution* (Princeton: Princeton University Press, 1984), p. 61. On the under-registration of deaths in early infancy, see also E. A. Wrigley, 'Births and baptisms: the use of Anglican baptism registers as a source of information about the numbers of births in England before the beginning of civil registration', *Population Studies* 31 (1977), pp. 281-312 especially p. 302, and Chris Galley, Naomi Williams and Robert Woods, 'Detection without correction: problems in assessing the quality of English ecclesiastical and civil registration', *Annales de Démographie Historique* (1995), pp. 161-183.

[23] William Farr, *English Life Table. Tables of Lifetimes, Annuities, and Premiums* (London: Longmans, Green and Co., 1864), and on age misreporting see R. D. Lee and D. Lam, 'Age distribution adjustments for English censuses, 1821 to 1931', *Population Studies* 37 (1983), pp. 445-464.

How reliable was the reporting of cause of death in Victorian times? Even today there is still considerable debate over the way in which cause is entered on the death certificate. Now the key problems relate to the definition of primary and secondary causes, and the variation in practice among certifying doctors between general practitioners and hospital doctors, and those cases in which an autopsy has been conducted as part of a coroner's inquest. In Victorian England and Wales many deaths were not certified by a member of the medical profession. This in itself would have posed certain problems for reliability, but its effects were also complicated: by the presence of distinct geographical variations in the percentage of deaths medically certified; the improvement in medical training which helped in the process of diagnosis; and the general expansion and professionalisation of the medical profession during the second half of the nineteenth century.[24] We have also to remember from Chapter 2 that nosologies changed, and that epidemiological and scientific knowledge was enhanced by significant advances in bacteriology.[25]

One possible way of exploring a particular aspect of the quality of cause of death registration by age and district is to focus on the Other causes category listed in Table 2. In highly effective and comprehensive nosologies the percentage of deaths placed in the residual category Other causes should be small and should not vary significantly with age, place or over time. To some extent this Other causes test would tend to reflect not only the ability of certifiers to state a classifiable cause, but also the number of categories in the nosology. This said, the result of the Other causes test appears to offer virtually the only opportunity to scrutinise one aspect of the quality of cause of death registration. The opportunity must not be missed, therefore.

Figure 8 considers the varying age profile of the percentage of deaths classified in the Other causes category in the *Decennial Supplements* for England and Wales from the 1850s to the 1890s. It shows, as one would expect from Figure 6, that between the age groups 5-9 and 55-64 the percentage is relatively low (about or less than 10 per cent), but among the deaths of those aged 0-4 and over 65 the percentage increases rapidly to about 25 in the first case and for deaths among the old to as much as 50 per cent. It is also clear from Figure 8 that the new nosology developed in the early 1880s by Dr William Ogle and applied retrospectively in the *Decennial Supplement* for the 1870s led to an increase in the percentage of deaths classified as Other causes in those very age groups where such percentages had been at their lowest. This may prove to be a serious problem for the comparison of decades.

[24] See Woods, 'Physician, heal thyself', for an account of the cause of death patterns among doctors themselves.
[25] W. F. Bynum, *Science and the Practice of Medicine in the Nineteenth Century* (Cambridge: Cambridge University Press, 1994), Roy Porter (ed.), *Cambridge Illustrated History of Medicine* (Cambridge: Cambridge University Press, 1996).

Figure 8. Percentage of deaths due to Other causes
by age groups, England and Wales, 1851-1860 to 1891-1900

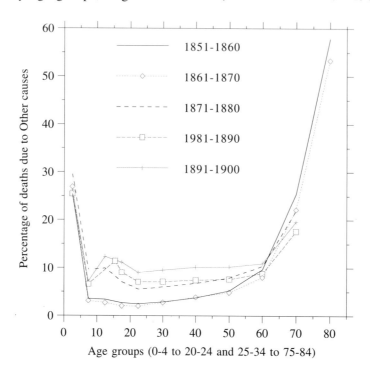

Figure 9. Percentage of deaths due to Other causes
by age in completed years (0-4), England and Wales,
1861-1870 to 1891-1900

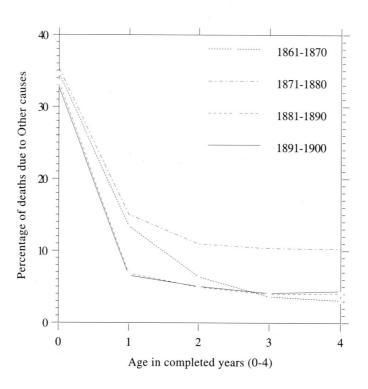

As is often the case, the age group 0-4 conceals wide variation between the experience of infants and other young children. Figure 9 illustrates this problem for the percentage of deaths due to Other causes for those who died aged 0, 1, 2, 3 and 4 in completed years. It shows that for infants between 30 and 35 per cent of deaths were so classified, but for those aged 2, 3 or 4 the percentage was closer to 5. Once again there is some variation between decades, but in this case the effects of epidemiological fortune may be more important than changes of nosology.

In sum, Figures 8 and 9 establish the point that although for infants and the old there are bound to be difficulties in using cause of death data simply because a substantial minority of deaths were not placed in distinct nosological categories; for those who died aged 1 to 65, from 85 to 95 per cent of causes were classified in the nosology used for the reporting of cause of death by age for registration districts in the *Decennial Supplements*.

Figure 10. Relationship between percentage of deaths due
to Other causes among infants and children
aged 1-4, and population density, England and Wales, 1861-1870

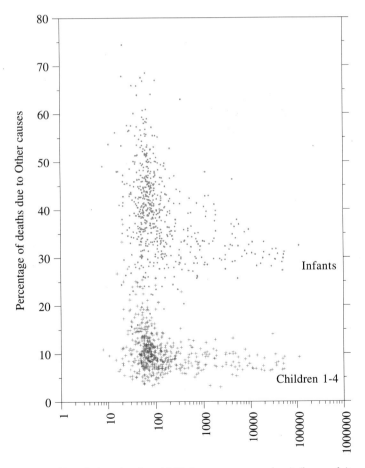

Population density, 1861 (persons per sq. km.) (log scale)

41

Of course this does not mean that either the certification or the classification will necessarily have been made correctly, but it does suggest that one should be extremely wary of using these geographically disaggregated cause of death data for infants and the old. However, it must be born in mind, and will have been obvious from Figure 2, that a very substantial proportion of all deaths in Victorian England occurred either to infants or the elderly. This may have serious implications for the wisdom of those attempts made to consider changes in cause of death structures without explicitly relating cause to age.[26]

The percentage of deaths placed in the residual Other causes category not only varied with age, but also geographically. Although in England and Wales 30 to 35 per cent of all infant deaths were so classified, many rural districts had 40, 50 and even 60 per cent of deaths placed in this category. Figure 10 clearly demonstrates that not all low population density and thus largely rural districts displayed this high Other causes percentage. Most of the populous urban districts fell into the 30 to 35 per cent range. The same pattern emerges for deaths in early childhood, but here the general level is lower and the range among rural districts far less.

Figure 11. Relationship between percentage of infant deaths due to Other causes and the population/ doctor ratio, England and Wales, 1861-1870

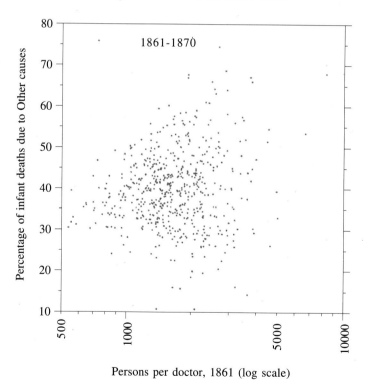

Persons per doctor, 1861 (log scale)

[26] As will be clear from Table 5 below, more detailed nosologies could be applied even in the case of infant deaths. In Ogle's tables only 2.6 and 4.4 per cent of infant deaths are classified as due to All other cause in the urban and rural areas, respectively (see Chapter 5).

It might be thought that the Other causes percentage reflects in some way the absence of medical practitioners capable of if not accurately, then at least consistently completing the death certificate in a way that would produce a classifiable cause of death for General Register Office statistics. But Figure 11 shows that there is no correspondence between Other causes for infants and the 1861 census based population/doctor ratio.

It should not come as a surprise that distinctive and persistent clusters of districts with high Other causes percentages existed in the nineteenth century and these are shown in Maps 4, 5 and 6.

Map 4, for example, shows that the percentage of infant deaths classified as from Other causes was both excessively and persistently high in the remoter parts of the far North of England, in East Anglia, mid-Wales and some parts of the south Midlands and the South West. It was relatively low in many of those districts dominated by the larger urban centres of the North, as well as parts of London, and was surprisingly low in both North and South Wales. Even with early childhood mortality mid-Wales, East Anglia, together with parts of the south Midlands, the South West and the North, display higher than average percentages for Other causes. Although Maps 4 and 5 are not strictly comparable because mean levels are substantially lower in the 1-4 age group and because early childhood mortality declined quite significantly between the 1860s and the 1890s whereas infant mortality did not.

Map 6 shows comparable percentages for those dying aged 65-74. In this case there are fewer distinct regional clusters, although the position of Wales seems to be anomalous once again especially in the 1860s. Maps 26 and 27 show Wales to have experienced relatively low mortality from Diseases of the Heart and the Brain in the 1860s. It seems more likely that such causes were avoided on death certificates for the old although as Maps 10 and 19 reveal Diseases of the Brain were especially prominent among infants and young children in Wales.

Clearly the matter of Other causes deaths poses several disturbing problems for any full account of the geography of demographic and epidemiological change in the nineteenth century. The suspicion must persist that there were local and perhaps regional variations in the quality of cause of death registration by age and district, although the extent cannot be precisely quantified. It appears that the safest ground lies in England and for deaths occurring to those aged between 1 and 65 years.

Map 4. Percentage of infant deaths due to Other causes

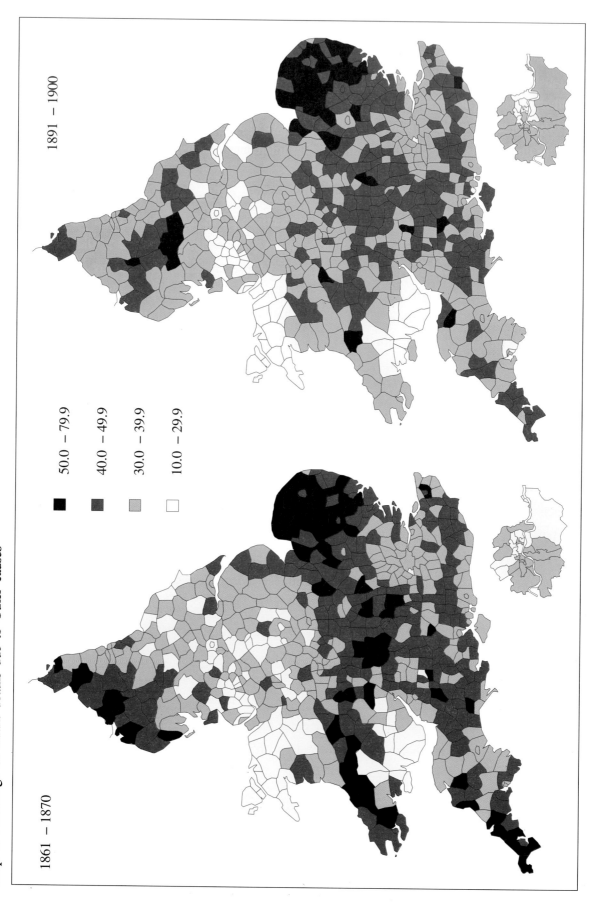

1861 – 1870

1891 – 1900

50.0 – 79.9

40.0 – 49.9

30.0 – 39.9

10.0 – 29.9

Map 5. Percentage of deaths aged 1 – 4 due to Other causes

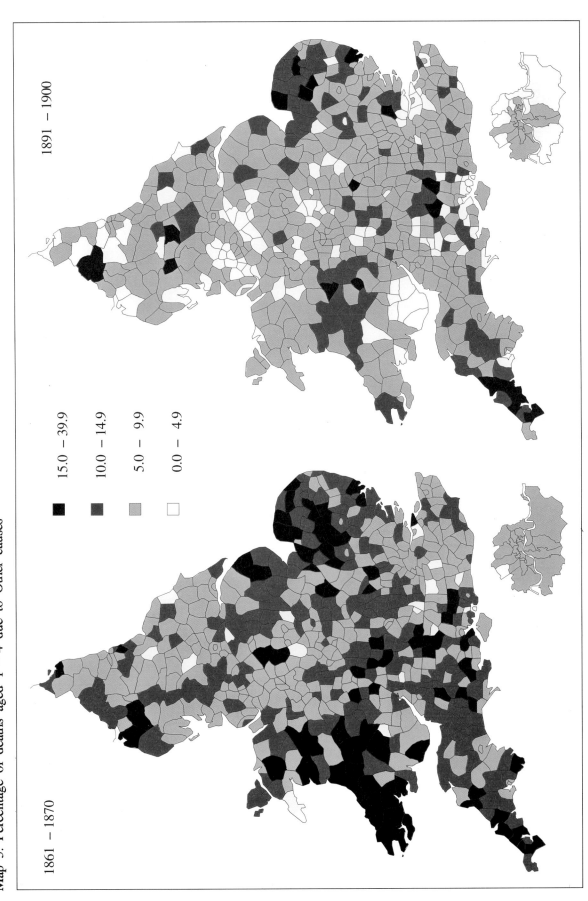

1891 – 1900

1861 – 1870

15.0 – 39.9

10.0 – 14.9

5.0 – 9.9

0.0 – 4.9

Map 6. Percentage of deaths aged 65 – 74 due to Other causes

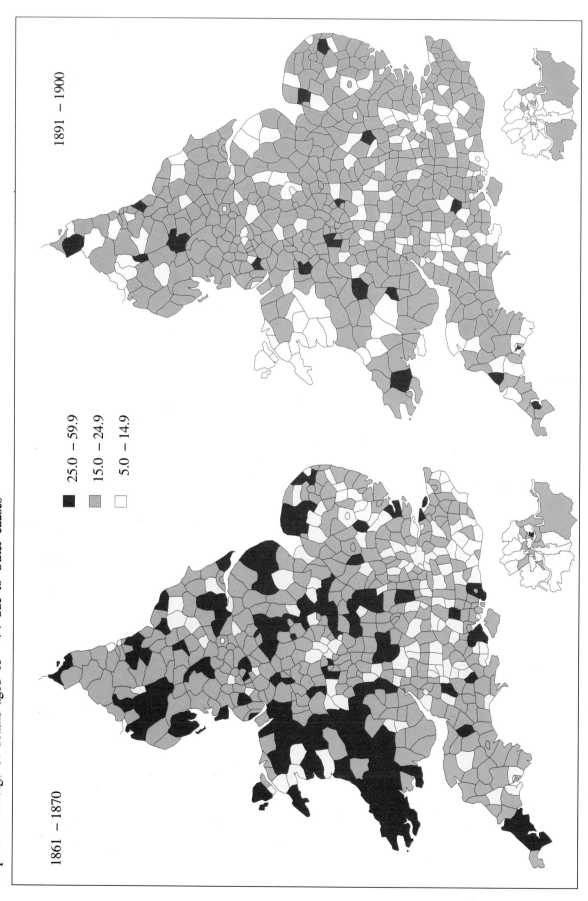

1861 – 1870

1891 – 1900

25.0 – 59.9
15.0 – 24.9
5.0 – 14.9

5

Infants

In Victorian England newly-born children were especially vulnerable to disease and early death. Their deaths represented upwards of 15 per cent of all deaths.[27] Although it is impossible to measure the extent of foetal loss and even to estimate the prevailing level of stillbirths is far from straightforward, each live birth should have been captured by the civil registration system as should each subsequent death including a record of the age at which the death occurred. The calculation of infant and early childhood mortality rates should be relatively simple, therefore. But the matter is made more complicated because of the suspicion that not all live births were registered, especially between 1837 and 1874, and that of those not recorded a substantial proportion was probably made up of infants who died in their first few hours or days of life and, further, that their deaths may also not have been registered. Any attempt to calculate the true infant mortality rate would need to adjust both the numerator (deaths of infants under 1 year of age) and the denominator (number of live births in a year), but for the purposes of this atlas the exercise would need to be performed on both a district and a decade-specific basis.[28] Clearly this is impossible without making a series of unjustifiable assumptions and no such corrections will be attempted here. It should also be born in mind that it terms of reported causes of death, infancy is one of the most troublesome age groups and that in many districts more than a third of such deaths were classified as due to Other causes (see Chapter 4 and especially Map 4).

However, since infant mortality is such an important contributor to overall mortality and a particularly sensitive indicator of the general health of a population it will be dealt with separately and in some detail despite the problems outlined above.

Table 4 uses the full English Life Tables to chart changes in the survival patterns of children. It shows that out of 1000 live births an increasing proportion did survive until age 10, but that there was little significant improvement in the survival chances of infants in their first year before the first decade of the twentieth century. The point is made far more clearly by Figure 12 which traces the annual rates for ages 0 (infancy) and 1-4 (early childhood), but also shows ages 1, 2, 3 and 4 separately. For England and Wales as

[27] R. I. Woods, P. A. Watterson and J. H. Woodward, 'The causes of rapid infant mortality decline in England and Wales, 1861-1921. Parts I and II', *Population Studies* 42 (1988), pp. 343-366 and 43 (1989), pp. 113-132, and Williams and Galley, 'Urban-rural differentials' surveys recent research on infant mortality in the nineteenth century. See also Hugh R. Jones, 'The perils and protection of infant life', *Journal of the Royal Statistical Society* 57 (1894), pp. 1-98 for an example of a detailed late-Victorian account, and Jalland, *Death in the Victorian Family*, pp. 119-142 on parental reactions to the deaths of infants and children.

[28] Galley *et al.*, 'Detection without correction' considers this problem at greater length.

Table 4. Survivors to ages 1 to 10 out of 1000 male and female (in italics) live births, England and Wales 1838-1854 to 1920-1922

Age	ELT 3 1838-1854		ELT 4 1871-1880		ELT 5 1881-1890		ELT 6 1891-1900		ELT 7 1901-1910		ELT 8 1910-1912		ELT 9 1920-1922	
1	836	*865*	841	*871*	839	*869*	828	*859*	856	*883*	880	*902*	910	*931*
2	783	*812*	790	*820*	791	*823*	784	*817*	821	*849*	849	*874*	889	*911*
3	755	*783*	764	*793*	772	*804*	768	*800*	808	*836*	838	*861*	879	*902*
4	737	*764*	746	*775*	760	*792*	758	*790*	799	*828*	831	*855*	873	*896*
5	724	*751*	734	*763*	751	*783*	750	*782*	794	*821*	826	*850*	870	*892*
6	714	*741*	727	*756*	745	*777*	745	*776*	790	*817*	822	*846*	866	*888*
7	706	*733*	721	*750*	741	*773*	741	*773*	787	*814*	819	*843*	863	*885*
8	700	*726*	716	*746*	738	*770*	738	*770*	784	*811*	816	*840*	861	*883*
9	694	*721*	712	*742*	735	*768*	736	*767*	782	*809*	814	*838*	859	*881*
10	690	*716*	709	*738*	733	*766*	734	*765*	781	*808*	812	*836*	857	*879*

Source: English Life Tables 3 to 9

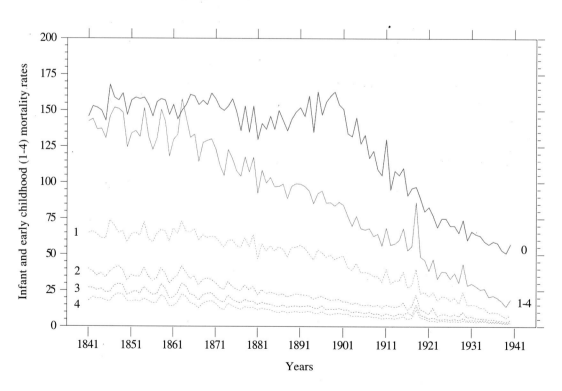

Figure 12. Annual IMR (0) and ECMR (1-4) series, England and Wales, 1841-1941 (q_1, q_2, q_3 and q_4 (all x 1000) are also shown)

Map 7a. Infant mortality rate, England and Wales

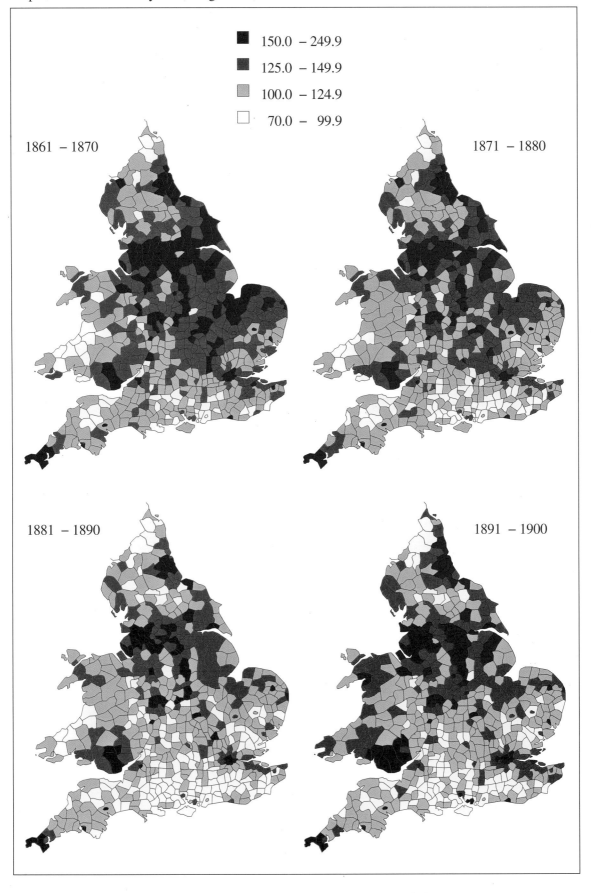

Map 7b. Infant mortality rate, London

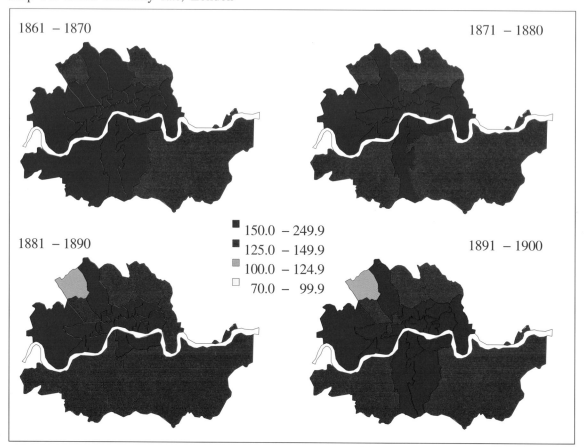

1861 — 1870

1871 — 1880

■ 150.0 — 249.9
■ 125.0 — 149.9
▨ 100.0 — 124.9
□ 70.0 — 99.9

1881 — 1890

1891 — 1900

a whole the infant mortality rate did not commence a secular decline until the turn of the twentieth century, but early childhood mortality was in decline, although initially volatile, from the 1860s onwards. This observation that infant and early childhood mortality displayed very different trends in the Victorian period is worth repeated emphasis because it reflects very different cause of death structures and this despite the fact that 12 months is no more than a convenient but arbitrary length of time in a child's early life upon which to base the calculation of such important demographic measures.[29]

As might be expected, IMR varied in a way that was far from uniform among the districts although the mean rate (about 150) and the range (about 70 to 250) changed little from decade to decade. Maps 7a and 7b show the variations in IMR among districts in the four decades for England and Wales, and London respectively. In broad terms the highest IMRs are to be found in urban areas and all urban areas have higher than average IMRs, but in the middle of the nineteenth century not all districts with high IMRs were urban. Scrutiny of Figure 4 in conjunction with Maps 7a and 7b reveals that whilst in, for example, the 1890s only a relatively small number of districts had IMRs above 150 they contained at least half the population of England and Wales. At the opposite end of the range, those districts with IMRs less than 100 were increasing in number, they were rural and remote or in the South of England, but they contained no more than 5 per cent of the population. What is especially interesting about these low mortality districts is that their existence confirms the ability of certain populations to achieve IMRs in the 80s and 90s well before the twentieth-century medical advances. There is also good reason to believe that in some rural parishes, in Devon for example, such low rates had existed for centuries and thus that they can be said to represent the minimum level of infant mortality attainable by a pre-industrial population in England.[30]

Interesting though these low mortality districts are, it is the high mortality districts which should command the most attention because it is these that have most influence on national rates. It is clear from Map 7a that in the 1860s there were districts round the Wash, in Lincolnshire and east Yorkshire, and in the west of Cornwall where IMR was higher than the national average, but where on the basis of a simple distinction between urban and rural districts one would have expected to find far lower rates. It also seems likely that these high IMRs had persisted for several centuries, at least in the eastern Fenlands near March and Gainsborough, and along the Thames Estuary. The larger industrial towns of the North and Midlands also showed persistently high IMRs, places like Liverpool, Manchester, Birmingham, Sheffield, Leeds and Newcastle, but some other smaller towns were also notorious for their high and in the 1890s rising IMRs (Preston

[29] Robert Woods, 'On the historical relationship between infant and adult mortality', *Population Studies* 47 (1993), pp. 195-219 considers in more detail the various age components of the mortality curve, especially infant and early childhood mortality.

[30] E. A. Wrigley *et al.*, *The Population History of England from Family Reconstitutions* (Cambridge: Cambridge University Press, 1997), especially Chapter 6 on mortality.

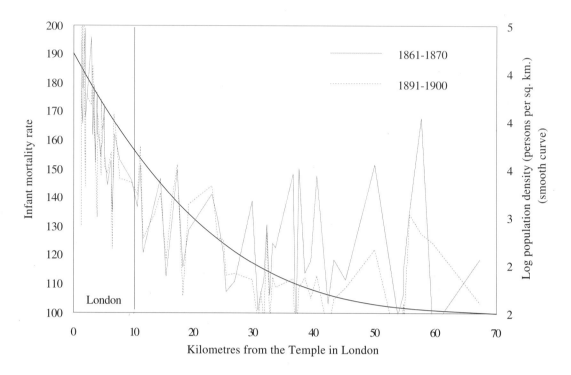

and Leicester, for example). But as Map 7a illustrates even those largely commercial urban centres that happened to wholly occupy single districts displayed IMRs in the highest category; places like Plymouth, Exeter, Southampton, Portsmouth, Brighton, Colchester and Norwich. And then there were the coalfield districts of South Wales, York-Derby-Notts., and County Durham each of which retained high IMRs well into the twentieth century.

Infant mortality for London as a whole also remained high by national standards, but was lower than many large provincial centres (Figure 7 sets London's cause of death pattern out in detail).[31] While IMR was above 150 in the central districts, those along the Thames and in the East End, but in the outer suburbs it remained at a lower level (Map 7b). (It was less than 125 in Hampstead even in the 1890s.) London provides an ideal opportunity not only to examine internal variations in mortality via the 25 districts used here, but also to reconstruct the particular form of an urban-rural mortality gradient. Figure 13 shows in a very simplified form the mortality gradient out from the centre of London for 70 kilometres. The IMR is plotted against distance from the Temple in central London. As would be expected, both mortality and population density decline with distance, and both the outer suburbs and the urban periphery show examples of IMR less

[31] See Williams and Mooney, 'Infant mortality', also Graham Mooney, *The Geography of Mortality Decline in Victorian London*, Unpublished PhD Thesis, University of Liverpool, 1994, and 'Did London pass the 'sanitary test'? Seasonal infant mortality in London, 1870-1914', *Journal of Historical Geography* 20 (1994), pp. 158-174.

than 150 in the 1860s and 1890s. It is also clear that some of the small towns located towards the edge of the 70 kilometre radius experienced high mortality, but not as high as some of the inner London districts.[32]

Maps 7a and 7b, in conjunction with Figures 12 and 13, help to draw a picture of limited change, but substantial geographical variation. This can be explored further using the cause of death data although, of course, special care must be taken in using such material for infants.

Figure 6 shows that in England and Wales the principal causes of death among infants were: Diseases of the Brain (Nervous system 1890s); Diseases of the Lung (Respiratory system 1890s) and Diarrhoea & Dysentery (also Diseases of the Digestive system 1890s). The special tables prepared by William Ogle for the *Fifty-fourth Annual Report* are summarised in Table 5. Ogle's intention was to illustrate the differences between urban and rural places in terms of their cause of death structures in infancy. He selected three high mortality towns—Blackburn, Leicester and Preston—which in combination had an IMR of 218 in 1889-1891 and three low mortality rural counties—Dorset, Hertfordshire and Wiltshire—with an IMR of only 97. For these urban and rural places he calculated life tables for infancy assuming 100,000 live births and then disaggregated the total infant deaths according to a specially devised nosology. The cumulative mortality rate during the first year of life is shown in Figure 14; it clearly demonstrates important differences between urban and rural environments in terms of the early age mortality curve.[33] Table 5 is important not only because it illustrates the differences between urban and rural environments in terms of infant mortality, but also because it shows the inadequacy of the nosology described in Table 2 where deaths under twelve months are concerned.[34] In Table 5 the principal causes of death in the urban places are: Diarrhoeal diseases, Convulsions and other Diseases of the Nervous system, Diseases of the Respiratory organs, Atrophy, Premature birth (75 per cent in total), and in the rural places they are: Diseases of the Respiratory organs, Atrophy, Convulsions and other Diseases of the Nervous system, Premature birth (68 per cent in total). The importance of Other causes for infant deaths in the Table 2 nosology compared with that of Table 5 is doubtless the result of

[32] See T. A. Welton, 'The effects of migration in disturbing local rates of mortality as exemplified in the statistics of London and the surrounding country for the years 1851-60', *Journal of the Institute of Actuaries* 16 (1872), pp. 153-186.

[33] Figure 14 is based on Ogle's Table C in the *Fifty-fourth Annual Report* for 1891 which provides an exceptionally detailed breakdown for age at death. See E. A. Wrigley, 'Births and baptisms'.. When the infant mortality rate is about 150, we estimate on the basis of extrapolation from twentieth-century experience that there will be approximately 45 stillbirths (over 28 weeks gestation) for every 1000 live births and the perinatal mortality rate will be about 100. See Graham Mooney, 'Still-births and the measurement of urban infant mortality rates c. 1890-1930', *Local Population Studies* 53 (1994), pp. 42-52.

[34] See Hallie J. Kintner, 'Classifying causes of death during the late nineteenth and early twentieth centuries: the case of German infant mortality', *Historical Methods* 19 (1986), pp. 45-54 for a detailed discussion of the various general problems to be faced in classifying cause of death for infants.

Table 5. Causes of death in infancy in three towns (U)—Blackburn, Leicester and Preston—and three rural counties (R)—Dorset, Hertfordshire and Wiltshire—of England, 1889-1891

Cause of death	Cumulative infant mortality rate from 100,000 live births up to the following ages:											
	1 week		1 month		3 months		6 months		9 months		12 months	
	U	R	U	R	U	R	U	R	U	R	U	R
Premature birth	1508	1020	2054	1267	2237	1340	2270	1369	2276	1375	2279	1381
Atelectasis	105	39	141	45	149	49	149	53	149	55	149	55
Congenital malformations	78	107	175	157	209	194	228	206	234	220	234	228
Whooping cough			12	17	94	100	263	204	490	304	694	416
Measles					20		69	13	263	81	626	176
Scarlet fever							3	2	14	4	31	6
Diarrhoeal diseases	3	4	189	39	1191	155	2606	322	3490	407	3961	481
Enteritis		6	22	21	152	43	296	75	428	103	497	122
Erysipelas			23	9	26	21	37	27	43	29	43	31
Syphilis	3	2	23	10	106	26	161	45	181	49	190	53
Liver disease	11	17	52	63	74	69	86	75	89	79	89	79
Dentition						2	86	24	228	100	424	187
Other Diseases of the Digestive organs	17	13	56	48	111	93	211	149	258	169	284	189
Convulsions and other Diseases of the Nervous system	435	233	901	444	1672	748	2673	1036	3348	1220	3776	1381
Tubercular meningitis	3		6	4	40	12	151	39	268	79	379	138
Tabes mesenterica	3		6	4	94	45	281	115	425	163	577	216
Other Tubercular diseases			3	8	53	16	142	40	200	89	261	118
Atrophy	360	579	862	968	1607	1329	2276	1564	2561	1675	2734	1738
Diseases of the Respiratory organs	25	22	189	168	839	585	1754	1103	2723	1604	3701	2105
Injury at birth	3	7	3	9	3	9	3	9	3	9	3	9
Naval haemorrhage			11	13	14	13	14	13	14	13	14	13
Suffocation	17	14	42	34	134	73	217	101	226	111	232	113
Other violence	8	33	11	38	19	38	26	43	34	48	51	54
All Other causes	67	67	166	122	282	220	424	305	499	366	574	428
All causes	2646	2163	4947	3488	9126	5180	14426	6932	18444	8352	21803	9717

Notes: Atelectasis—an imperfect expansion of the lung at birth, Erysipelas—an infectious inflammation of the skin, Atrophy—wasting. Definitions from Payne, *Pocket Vocabulary*. The original tables were prepared by Dr. William Ogle using death certificates.

Source: Registrar General's *Fifty-fourth Annual Report* for 1891, Tables D and E, pp. xiv-xv (see Appendix 1).

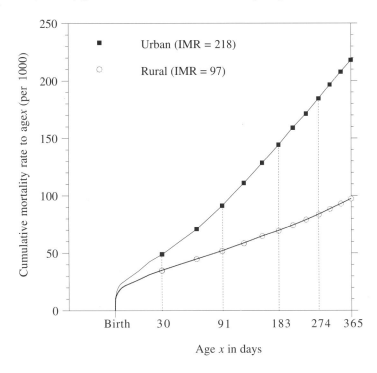

Figure 14. Cumulative mortality rate during the first year of life for three towns (Urban) and three counties (Rural) of England, 1889-1891 (age x has been transformed by $\log^3 (x +1)$)

including such causes as Premature birth which is recorded separately in Table 5. The importance of Diarrhoeal diseases in the three towns is also especially noteworthy because of its contribution to post-neonatal mortality and this is also reflected in Figure 14 where infant mortality after 1, 3, 6 and 9 months is highlighted.

Let us begin to consider cause of death in infancy by dealing with the case of Diarrhoea & Dysentery and do so by considering its varying influence in conjunction with that of urbanisation as measured by population density. Figure 15, and in greater detail Figure 16, helps to set the scene. The infant mortality rate and population density are of course closely related, but not perfectly so. One of the elements of IMR—Diarrhoea & Dysentery—clearly behaves in a way that whilst sensitive to population density does not always show additional increases beyond a particular density threshold (approximately 200 persons per square kilometre). This tends to suggest that although sparsely populated rural districts are likely to have low rates of Diarrhoea & Dysentery IMR, small towns and large cities may have much higher, but similar rates. In other words, the process of urban growth that turns a village into a town may have a larger impact on increasing IMR via Diarrhoea & Dysentery than that process would have were it to continue and turn the town into a large city. Further, once the majority of the population of a country is living in places with densities above the threshold then the effects of

55

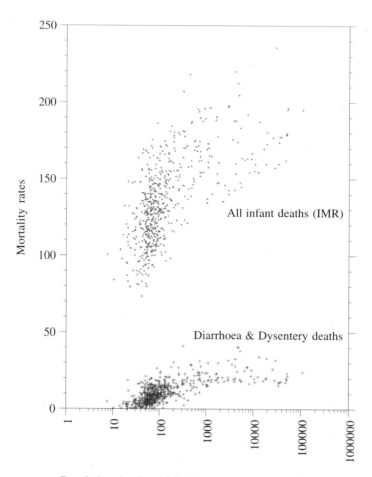

Figure 15. Relationship between total infant mortality
and Diarrhoea & Dysentery infant mortality rates,
and population density, England and Wales, 1861-1870

Population density, 1861 (persons per sq. km.) (log scale)

additional urbanisation are likely to become muted at least in terms of sanitation sensitive
Diarrhoea & Dysentery and its effect on infant mortality.

In general, Figures 15 and 16 provide little evidence that the Victorian sanitary
revolution had a major demographic impact in the nineteenth century, at least among
infants.[35] However, Figure 16 (also Map 8b) does reveal that in the 1890s a handful of
districts (all in London, and despite more general deterioration) did show far lower
Diarrhoea & Dysentery IMR than one would expect on the basis of population density
and compared with what was possible in the 1860s. But Figure 17 tells a rather different
story, even for the 1890s, about Birmingham Borough.[36] It plots the number of infant
deaths and deaths from diarrhoea (most but not all of which would have been among

[35] See Woods *et al.*, 'Causes of infant mortality', especially Part I, and the concerns of contemporaries about
the increase of IMR in the 1890s (also shown in Figure 12).

[36] The case of Birmingham is dealt with in far greater detail in Robert Woods, 'Mortality and sanitary
conditions in late-nineteenth-century Birmingham', in Robert Woods and John Woodward (eds.) *Urban
Disease and Mortality in Nineteenth-Century England* (London: Batsford, 1984), pp. 176-202. Note that
this material relates to the Borough of Birmingham and not the Birmingham registration district.

Figure 16. Relationship between Diarrhoea & Dysentery
infant mortality rate and population density,
England and Wales, 1861-1870 and 1891-1900

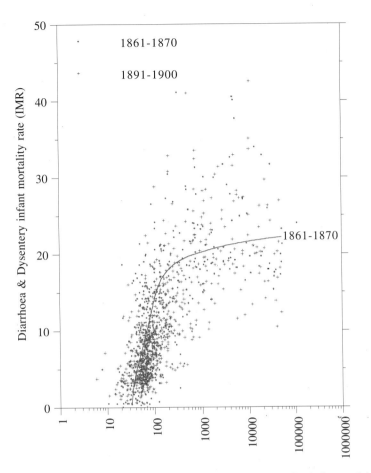

Population density, 1861 or 1891 (persons per sq. km.) (log scale)

infants by weeks for the years 1880-1901.[37] The incidence of summer infant diarrhoea was clearly of very considerable importance in influencing the annual rate of infant mortality and for Birmingham in the 1890s this particular element of early age mortality was even more important than it had been in earlier decades and certainly the 1880s. The significance of summer peaks for infant mortality rates is also illustrated by Figure 18 which, again for Birmingham, shows the median and the range of infant deaths that occurred in each of the 52 weeks of the year for those same 22 years used in Figure 17. The worst case scenario would have each week of a hypothetical year experience the highest number of infant deaths recorded in any of the 22 years—this would give an IMR of 332—while the best case would produce an IMR of only 109.[38] The infant mortality rate actually experienced in Birmingham in this period was closer to 180. The importance

[37] These time-series have been smoothed using a 9-point moving mean. The effect is to create a smoother curve with many minor and short-term variations removed.

[38] It must be remembered that this is an entirely hypothetical exercise, but it is nonetheless useful in establishing the range of IMR experience which a large Victorian city might have encountered. When combined with the evidence in Figure 14 and Table 5 it emphasises the seasonal dimension of high post-neonatal mortality in urban environments.

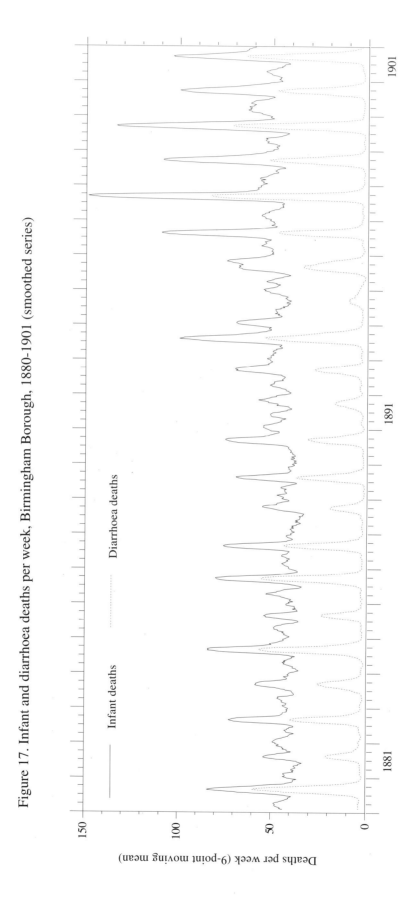

Figure 17. Infant and diarrhoea deaths per week, Birmingham Borough, 1880-1901 (smoothed series)

58

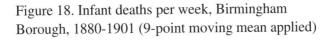

Figure 18. Infant deaths per week, Birmingham
Borough, 1880-1901 (9-point moving mean applied)

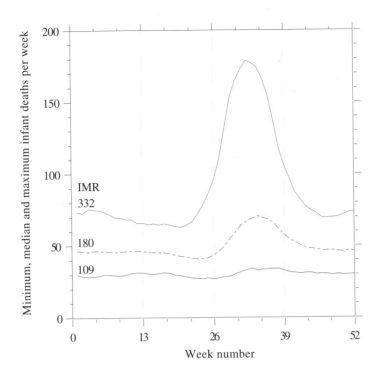

of this exercise is that it illustrates the points that, first, even if every week had been a 'good week' in late Victorian Birmingham then infant mortality would still have been higher than in many of the rural districts of the South of England (see Map 7a and Table 5) and, second, what turned a 'good year' into a 'very bad year' was largely a matter of the height, but also the basal width (at worst June to October inclusive) of the summer mortality peak.

Maps 8a and 8b show the distribution of Diarrhoea & Dysentery IMR in the four decades. In broad terms there are strong similarities between decades, although more districts have lower rates in the 1880s, and it is of course the urban places that consistently have the highest rates. At the other end of the range there are districts with rates consistently less than 5 per thousand, in parts of south west Wales and the northern Pennines, for example.

Map 9 compares Diseases of the Lung for the 1860s with Diseases of the Respiratory system IMR for the 1890s. The result is troubling in terms of the implications it suggests for cause of death registration and the effects changes of nosology may have had, but it may also suggest that mortality from this broad category of diseases was indeed higher for infants in the 1890s than the 1860s.

Similarly, Map 10 compares Diseases of the Brain for the 1860s with Diseases of the Nervous system IMR for the 1890s. Here there is rather more correspondence, with North

Map 8a. Diarrhoea & Dysentery infant mortality rate, England and Wales

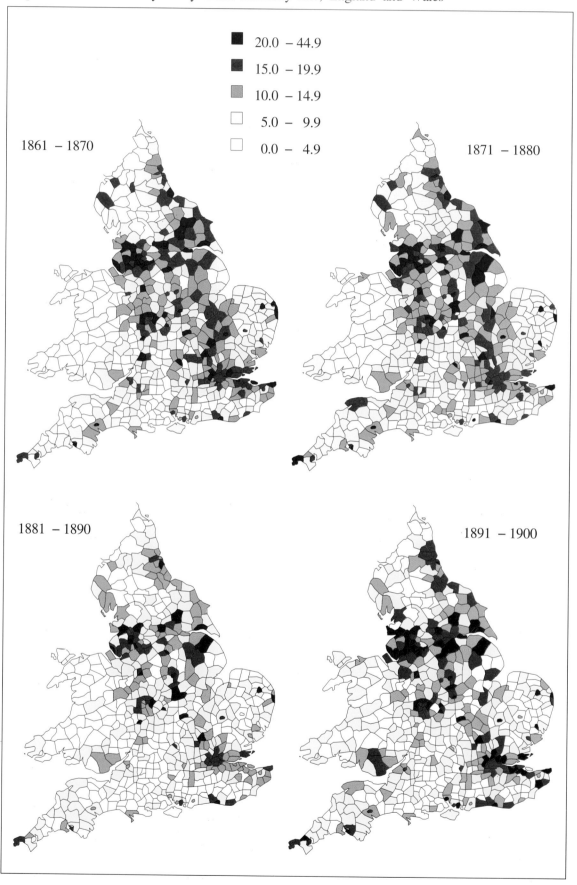

■ 20.0 – 44.9
■ 15.0 – 19.9
▨ 10.0 – 14.9
□ 5.0 – 9.9
□ 0.0 – 4.9

1861 – 1870

1871 – 1880

1881 – 1890

1891 – 1900

Map 8b. Diarrhoea & Dysentery infant mortality rate, London

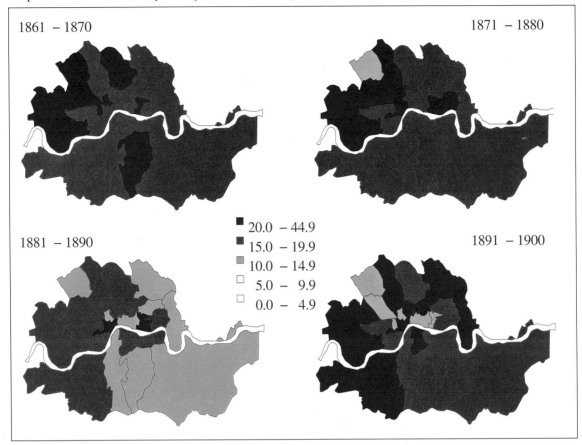

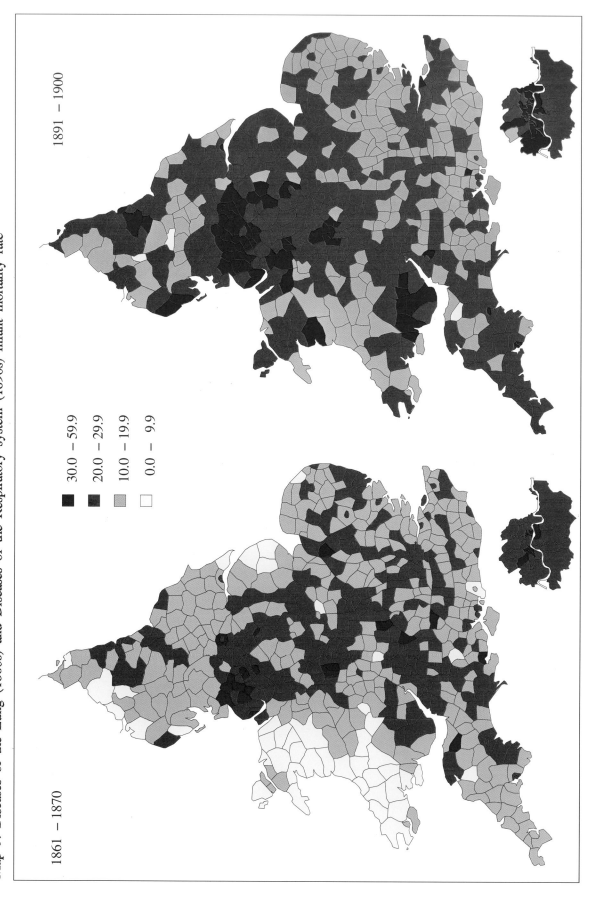

Map 9. Diseases of the Lung (1860s) and Diseases of the Respiratory system (1890s) infant mortality rate

1861 – 1870

1891 – 1900

30.0 – 59.9
20.0 – 29.9
10.0 – 19.9
0.0 – 9.9

Map 10. Diseases of the Brain (1860s) and Diseases of the Nervous system (1890s) infant mortality rate

1891 – 1900

40.0 – 89.9

20.0 – 39.9

10.0 – 19.9

0.0 – 9.9

1861 – 1870

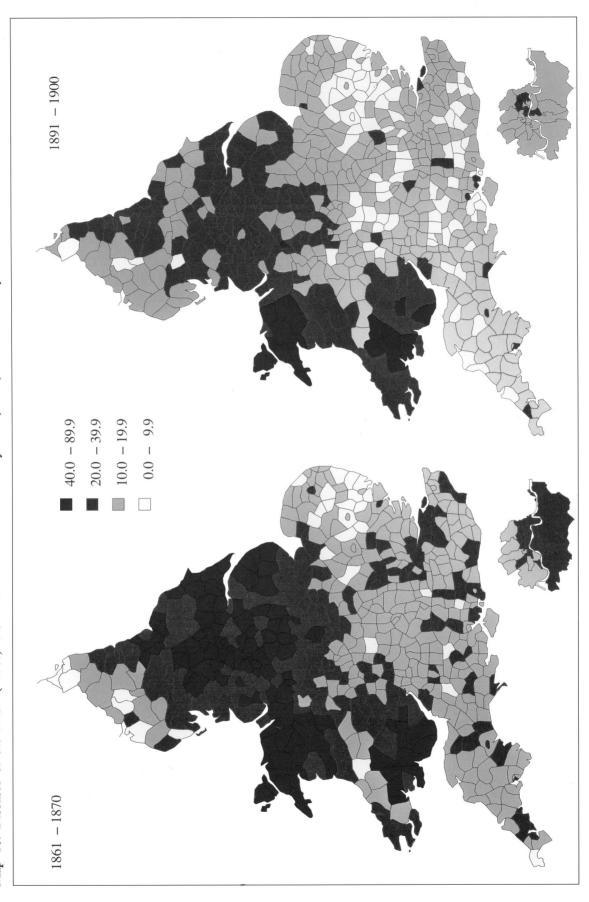

and South Wales, and the North of England containing districts with the worst rates in both decades.

Apart from the problems related to the relatively high and variable Other causes category, infant mortality in late nineteenth-century England and Wales can be shown to display the following features: the national rate stayed at a high level throughout; geographical variations drew sharp distinctions between urban and rural districts; and diseases like diarrhoea, dysentery and respiratory diseases played an important part in creating a particularly dangerous urban epidemiological environment.

6

Young children

Most of this chapter is devoted to a consideration of the life chances and cause of death patterns affecting those young children who reached their first birthday, but did not survive to their fifth. That is, it focuses on the early childhood mortality rate (ECMR, ages 1 to 4 in completed years), which is measured by the probability of dying between exact age 1 and age 5 (i.e. the life table function $_4q_1$ x 1000). We have already seen in Figure 12 that ECMR was in decline from mid-century and thus that it showed a very different trend from that of IMR. It is also clear from Figure 12 that early childhood mortality experienced some violent fluctuations especially in the 1850s and 1860s, but that thereafter the perturbations subsided only to be broken by the great influenza pandemic of 1918-1919. There is also some evidence from elsewhere in Europe that childhood mortality increased from early to mid-century and that some of the infectious diseases— especially scarlet fever, measles and whooping cough—were prominent in the 1850s and 1860s in the cities.[39] While being inherently interesting, the mortality experienced by the age group 1 to 4 is also of special significance because it was in decline when mortality in infancy was not (see also Figure 2). The progress of ECMR decline was of fundamental importance for the general decline of mortality and slow increase in life expectancy at birth especially in the nineteenth century. For these reasons, and because the Other causes category was far lower among young children than infants, early childhood mortality will receive special attention in this atlas.

It is also worth bearing in mind at the outset that while members of the Victorian medical profession found it relatively easy to distinguish between the various infectious diseases of childhood, as may have parents, the full aetiologies of these common diseases were not accurately described until the twentieth century. Further, that therapeutic measures for infants and young children were to say the least rudimentary if not actually harmful to life. For example Dr Charles West, one of the country's leading authorities on the care of children, offers the following opinion in his celebrated *Lectures on the Diseases of Infancy and Childhood* (seventh edition, 1884), 'I am always averse to the common practice of giving small quantities of opium, at short intervals, for the purpose of checking diarrhoea or of soothing restlessness in young infants; and prefer, unless there

---

[39] Gunnar Fridlizius, 'The deformation of cohorts: nineteenth-century mortality decline in a generational perspective', *Scandinavian Economic History Review* 37 (1989), pp. 3-17 provides evidence especially for Stockholm, see also Woods, 'Historical relationship'.

be some strong reason to the contrary, to give a larger dose of the remedy once or twice in the twenty-four hours' (p. 23).[40]

Let us begin by establishing the extent of geographical variation in ECMR and then consider what changes were evident in the period. It is clear from Maps 11a and 11b and Figure 5 that there were indeed very distinct geographical variations, but that in general and once again the principal distinction to be drawn is that between urban and rural districts. Map 11a suggests that the fit is not perfect, however. For example, the South West of England and the west of Wales retain rather higher ECMRs in the 1890s than one might expect of essentially rural, low population density areas although there has been decline since mid-century. The dramatic nature of the decline is conveyed by Figure 5 which shows the percentage of the population of England and Wales living in districts with given levels of early childhood mortality. Although the minimum level of ECMR does not alter substantially, a far higher proportion of the population was living in districts towards the lower end of the range in the 1890s than in the 1860s. This is also evident from Map 11. A little more of the regularity of pattern and its change may be discerned from Figure 19 where ECMRs are simply plotted against population density. In the 1860s 72 per cent of the variation in ECMR could be associated with population density while in the 1890s the figure was 64 per cent, but of greater interest are the positions and slopes of the regression lines that summarise the two relationships. The most substantial absolute and relative decline in ECMR came in those districts with the highest rates in the 1860s and these were, of course, also the districts with the highest population densities. Although ECMR did decline in many rural districts, its decline in the populous cities was instrumental in assisting the general rise in life expectancy.[41] However, Figure 19 also shows that certain high population density districts retained high ECMRs in a way that may prove to reflect more on the location of isolation hospitals than the distribution

[40] West, *Lectures*. West's lectures were first published in 1848 and offer a marvellous summary of the development of Victorian paediatrics including notes on the administration of leeches, mercury, antimony and as above opium. Nourishment, careful nursing and good ventilation were the best remedies, however. This is the general approach taken by other health manuals of the time, see for example, Thomas Bull, *The Maternal Management of Children in Health and Disease* (London: Longman, Green, Longman, and Robert, seventh edition 1861).

[41] Robert Woods, Naomi Williams and Chris Galley, 'Differential mortality patterns among infants and other young children: the experience of England and Wales in the nineteenth century', in Carlo A Corsini and Pier Paolo Viazzo (eds.) *The Decline of Infant and Child Mortality: The European Experience, 1750-1990* (The Hague: Kluwer, 1997), pp. 57-72 provides a more detailed account of the differences between infant and early childhood mortality. See also, Jeremiah M. Sullivan, Shea Oscar Rutstein and George T. Bicego, *Infant and Child Mortality, Demographic and Health Surveys Comparative Studies No. 15* (Calverton, Maryland: Macro International Inc., 1994).

Map 11a. Early childhood mortality rate ages 1 – 4, England and Wales

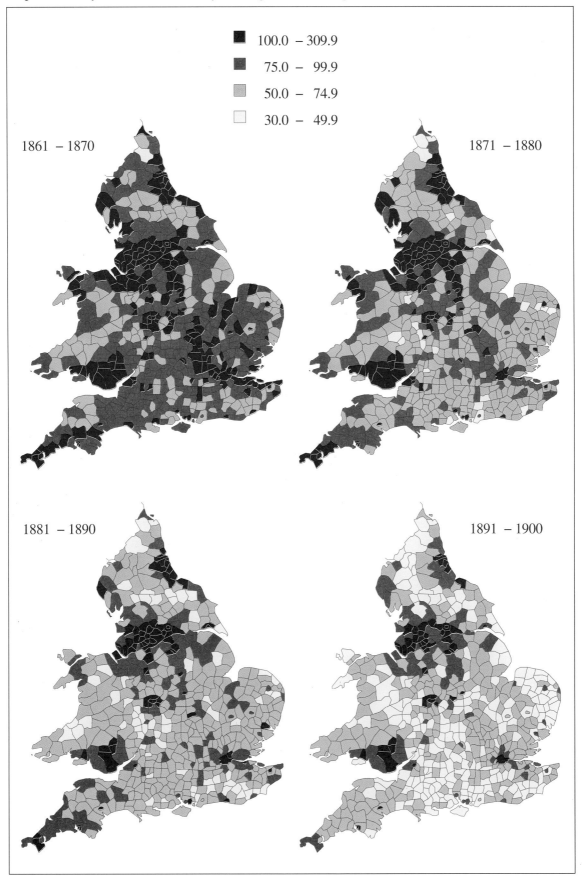

Map 11b. Early childhood mortality rate ages 1 − 4, London

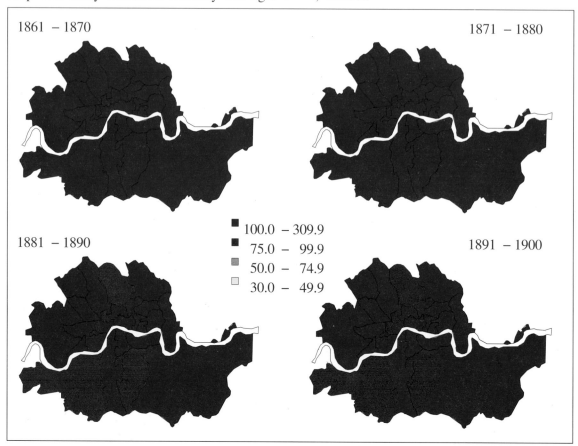

1861 − 1870

1871 − 1880

1881 − 1890

1891 − 1900

■ 100.0 − 309.9
■ 75.0 − 99.9
■ 50.0 − 74.9
□ 30.0 − 49.9

Figure 19. Relationship between early childhood mortality rate (ECMR)
and population density, England and Wales, 1861-1870 and 1891-1900

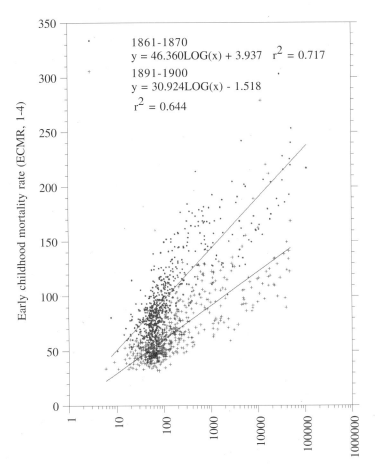

1861-1870
y = 46.360LOG(x) + 3.937 r^2 = 0.717

1891-1900
y = 30.924LOG(x) - 1.518
r^2 = 0.644

Population density, 1861 or 1891 (persons per sq. km.) (log scale)

of any specially lethal diseases.[42]

Maps 11a and 11b need to be differentiated into constituent cause of death patterns
and as before this can be done using Figures 6 and 7. The childhood infectious diseases—
especially Measles, Scarlet fever, Whooping cough and Diphtheria in the 1890s—stand
out as being particularly important alongside Diseases of the Brain (Nervous system
1890s) and Diseases of the Lung (Respiratory system 1890s). Mortality in early
childhood is clearly dominated by the common infectious diseases of childhood,

---

[42] The presence of workhouses, asylums, general hospitals, isolation hospitals or sanatoria in districts can
distort the mortality patterns when deaths are not recorded by usual place of residence. This may be an
important problem in certain London districts and for county towns with large workhouses, prisons or
garrisons. Mooney, *Mortality Decline in Victorian London*, Table 3.8, shows that between 1851 and 1901
the percentage of deaths in London occurring in institutions rose from 16 to 31. Victorian civil
registration does not allow this problem to be corrected easily, although some attempt seems to have been
made to re-allocate deaths even in the 1890s, not until 1911 was this done as a matter of course. See Higgs,
'Statistical Big Bang', pp. 421-425. Isolation policy also became an important medical issue; see, for
example, Arthur Newsholme, 'The utility of isolation hospitals in diminishing the spread of scarlet fever',
Journal of Hygiene 1 (1901), pp. 145-152, and John M. Eyler, 'Scarlet fever and confinement: the
Edwardian debate over isolation hospitals', *Bulletin of the History of Medicine* 61 (1987), pp. 1-24.

Map 12a. Diarrhoea & Dysentery early childhood mortality rate ages 1 – 4, England and Wales

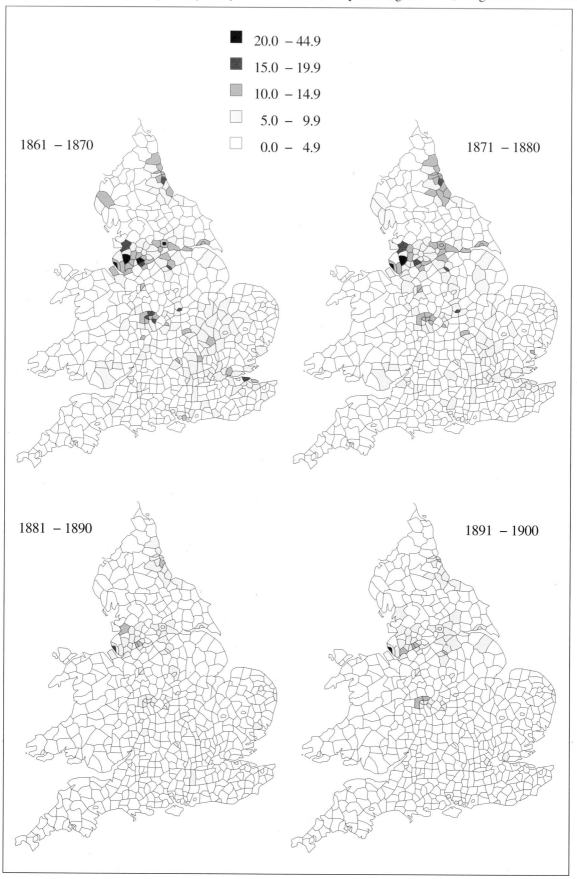

20.0 – 44.9
15.0 – 19.9
10.0 – 14.9
5.0 – 9.9
0.0 – 4.9

1861 – 1870

1871 – 1880

1881 – 1890

1891 – 1900

Map 12b. Diarrhoea & Dysentery early child mortality rate ages 1 – 4, London

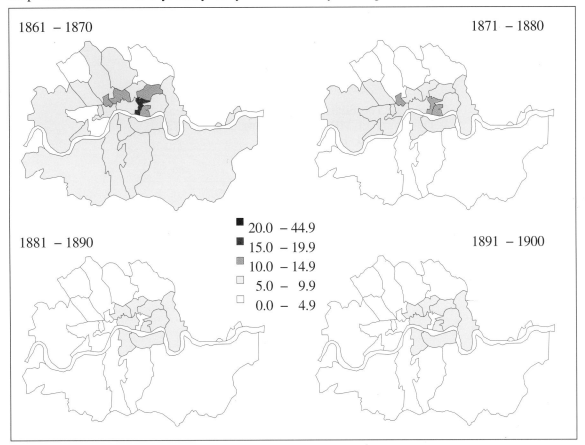

1861 – 1870

1871 – 1880

1881 – 1890

1891 – 1900

■ 20.0 – 44.9
■ 15.0 – 19.9
■ 10.0 – 14.9
□ 5.0 – 9.9
□ 0.0 – 4.9

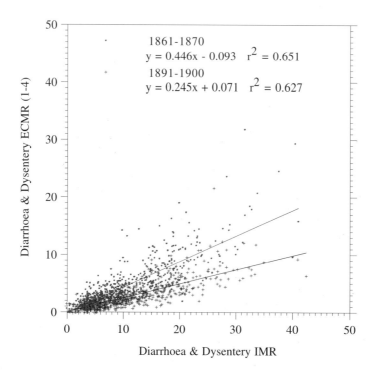

Figure 20. The relationship between Diarrhoea
& Dysentery ECMR and IMR, England and Wales,
1861-1870 and 1891-1900

1861-1870
$y = 0.446x - 0.093 \quad r^2 = 0.651$

1891-1900
$y = 0.245x + 0.071 \quad r^2 = 0.627$

Diarrhoea & Dysentery ECMR (1-4)

Diarrhoea & Dysentery IMR

which were all great killers in the Victorian period, and respiratory diseases. These causes of death will therefore receive most attention in this chapter. However, before we turn to these prominent causes of death let us consider two more minor, but nonetheless interesting contributors to early age mortality: Diarrhoea & Dysentery and Smallpox.

The early childhood mortality rate from Diarrhoea & Dysentery was lower than for infancy and its relative contribution much lower, although it should be noted that Diseases of the Digestive system were quite prominent in the 1890s and that it is possible that the causes reported on some death certificates were classified under that heading in later decades of the nineteenth century. Maps 12a and 12b show the distribution of Diarrhoea & Dysentery ECMR and Figure 20 compares the distributions of early childhood with infant Diarrhoea & Dysentery rates in the 1860s and 1890s. As would be expected, there is a close association between the two rates in each decade, but the general decline in the 1-4 rate compared with the rate for infants is obvious. Map 12a reinforces the point that Diarrhoea & Dysentery ECMR declined virtually everywhere although its relative distribution still tended to follow the most urbanised areas of the country. Clearly there are matters to be explained here because the 1890s, for example, were characterised by a national increase in mortality from the diarrhoeal diseases among infants.[43]

The case of smallpox is well known to medical historians and provides perhaps the best early example of how medical science when supported by public health measures could have a direct bearing on the health and life chances of the population. Although the demographic impact of further decline in mortality from smallpox was not great in the late nineteenth century, the geographical distribution of the disease and its further progress towards controlled extinction is interesting in its own right.[44] Map 13 focuses on early childhood mortality, an age group formerly important for smallpox deaths, and shows how by the 1890s the risk of dying had become zero in most parts of the country, but that there were still some important outbreaks (Gloucester in the 1890s) and districts where the vaccination programme had either been not entirely effective or where there was resistance to vaccination (Leicester in the 1860s and 1870s). Map 13 illustrates one of the nineteenth century's most successful stories as far as preventive medicine is concerned.

Let us return now to those infectious diseases still lethal to young children in Victorian England: measles, whooping cough, scarlet fever and diphtheria. The Birmingham example of the 1880s and 1890s illustrates just how important these four diseases were in combination not only for the level of mortality among those aged 1-4, but also the extent to which short-run temporal variations are affected (see Figure 21). It also warns us to be mindful of the periodicity of epidemics when using data defined arbitrarily in terms of decades.[45]

---

[43] One possible explanation for the difference in behaviour of the infant and early childhood mortality from Diarrhoea & Dysentery is that there was some downward drift in the average age at weaning in the late nineteenth century from say 14 months to 9-10 months. This would have had the effect of placing one of the most vulnerable periods of early life in the first rather than the second year. Unfortunately, very little is known about changes in the duration or intensity of breastfeeding in this period, see Woods *et al.*, 'Causes of infant mortality', Part II.

[44] See Naomi Williams, 'The implementation of compulsory health legislation: infant smallpox vaccination in England and Wales, 1840-1890', *Journal of Historical Geography* 20 (1994), pp. 396-412.

[45] Anne Hardy, *The Epidemic Streets: Infectious Disease and the Rise of Preventive Medicine, 1856-1900* (Oxford: Clarendon Press, 1993) provides a very valuable account of the historical epidemiology of childhood infectious diseases with a particular emphasis on Victorian London. See also Roy M. Anderson and Robert M. May, *Infectious Diseases of Humans: Dynamics and Control* (Oxford: Oxford University Press, 1992) especially pp. 130-134 on measles and whooping cough control since the 1940s.

Map 13. Smallpox early childhood mortality rate ages 1 – 4

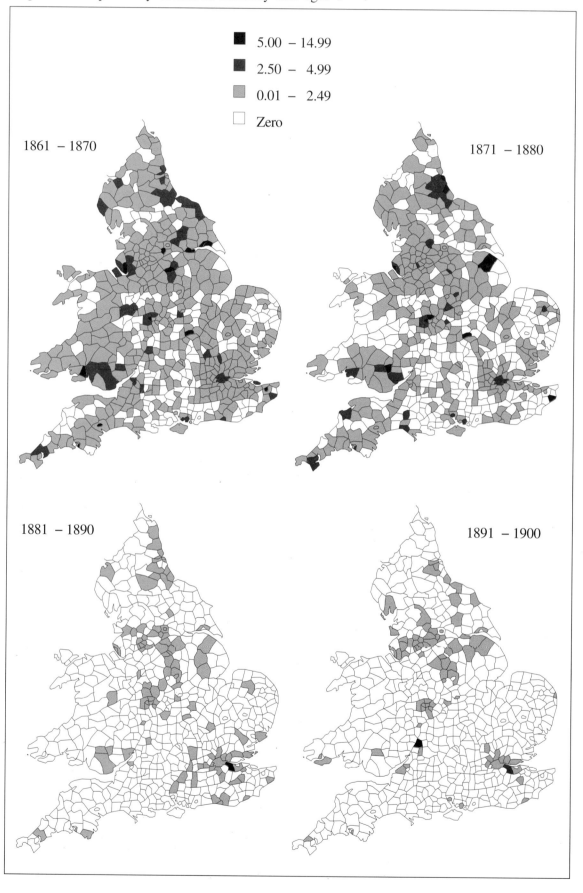

5.00 – 14.99
2.50 – 4.99
0.01 – 2.49
Zero

1861 – 1870

1871 – 1880

1881 – 1890

1891 – 1900

Figure 21. Deaths aged 1-4 and deaths from measles, whooping cough, scarlet fever and diphtheria per week, Birmingham Borough, 1880-1901 (smoothed series)

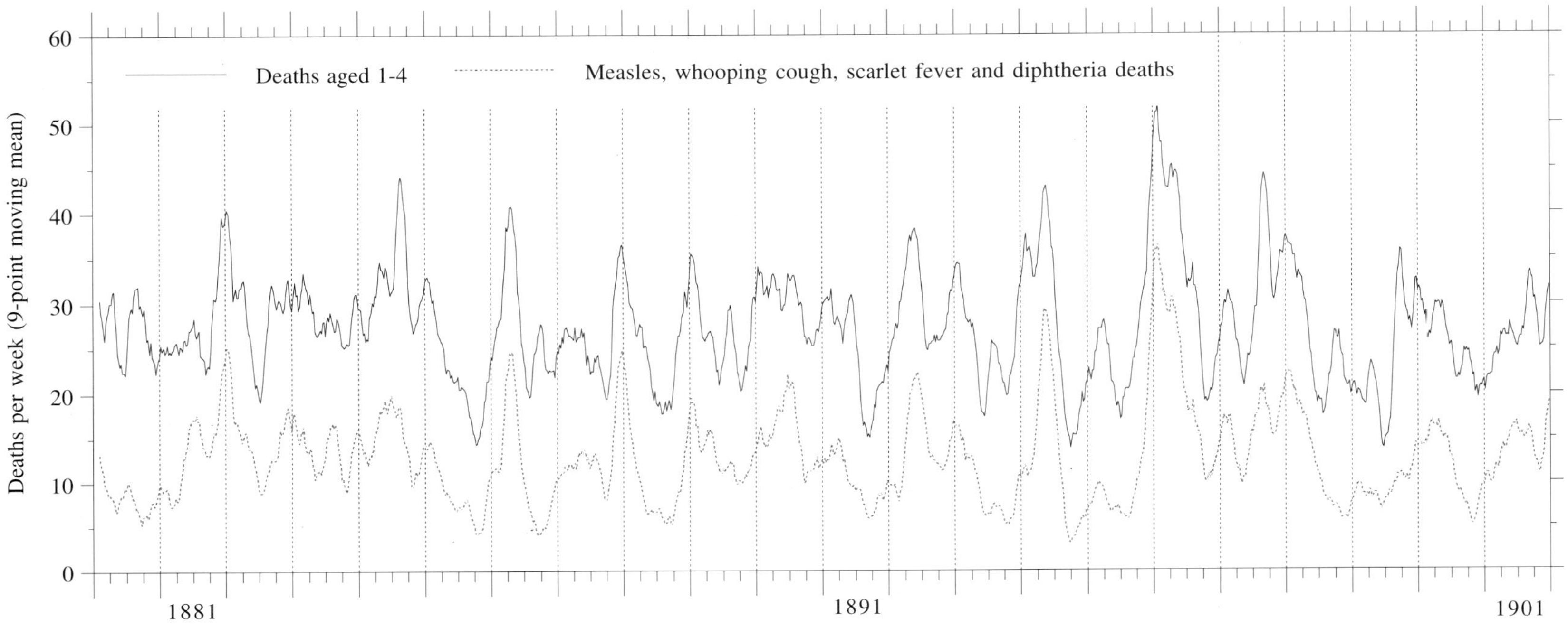

75

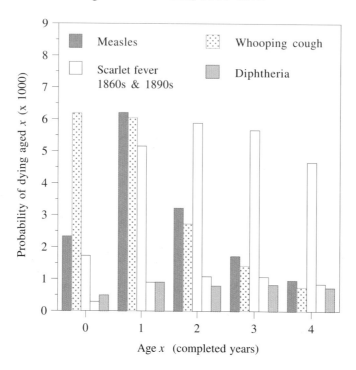

Figure 22. Age-specific mortality profiles for the infectious diseases of childhood, England and Wales, 1861-1870

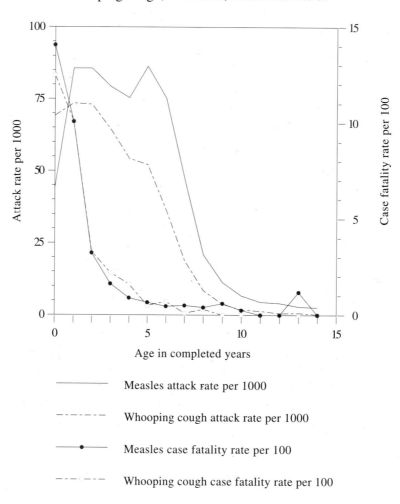

Figure 23. Attack and case fatality rates for measles and whooping cough, Aberdeen, 1880s and 1890s

———————— Measles attack rate per 1000

– – – – – – Whooping cough attack rate per 1000

—•—•— Measles case fatality rate per 100

–·–·–·– Whooping cough case fatality rate per 100

76

Figure 22 shows the under-five age-specific mortality profiles for these four diseases in the 1860s for England and Wales. In infancy Whooping cough dominates, although its position is matched by Measles and Scarlet fever in the second year of life. In the 1860s Scarlet fever dominates in years three to five, but by the 1890s mortality in these years has fallen to the level of that due to Diphtheria. In terms of the age pattern of mortality, Figure 22 encourages the traditional pairing: measles with whooping cough, and scarlet fever with diphtheria.[46]

Measles and whooping cough appear to have operated in tandem. As far as can be judged from studies undertaken in Aberdeen on data for both cases and deaths, the age profile of the case fatality rates for measles and whooping cough were similar although the age-specific attack rate differed somewhat (Figure 23).[47] Work on the periodicity of epidemics of the two diseases illustrates the two-yearly and alternating cycles; the case of Birmingham being no exception (Figure 24).[48]

Early childhood mortality caused by Measles was persistently highly sensitive to variations in population density, even more so than was Diarrhoea & Dysentery, throughout the nineteenth century. This is clearly shown by Figure 25, which should be compared with Figure 16. The growth of population and its additional concentration in a relatively small number of districts would undoubtedly have led to a national increase in the measles mortality rate perhaps throughout the eighteenth and early nineteenth centuries. Maps 14a and 14b only serve to emphasise the same point in terms of spatial variations for the Victorian era. They also show that whilst there was a high degree of correspondence between the four decades, there were also some interesting variations which in the case of the coalfield areas of York-Derby-Notts. and its higher rate of Measles mortality by the 1890s was a simple reflection of increased population density, but for other parts of the country the random nature of measles epidemics was probably of more importance: Weymouth in the 1880s, for example.[49]

[46] Scarlet fever and diphtheria were not separated in standard nosologies until 1856.

[47] Figure 23 is based on the findings of James S. Laing, 'Whooping cough: its prevalence and mortality in Aberdeen', *Public Health* 14 (10) (1902), pp. 584-99, and George N. Wilson, 'Measles: its prevalence and mortality in Aberdeen', *Public Health* 18 (2) (1905), pp. 65-82. Early accounts of the 'epidemic wave' are to be found in Arthur Ransome, 'On the form of the epidemic wave, and some of its probable causes', *Transactions of the Epidemiological Society* 1 (1881-1882), pp. 96-107; A. Campbell Munro, 'Measles: an epidemiological study', *Transactions of the Epidemiological Society* 10 (1890-1891), pp. 94-109; B. Arthur Whitelegge, 'Measles epidemics, major and minor', *Transactions of the Epidemiological Society* 12 (1892-1893), pp. 37-54.

[48] Again, compare John Brownlee, 'Periodicities of epidemics of measles in the large towns of Great Britain and Ireland', *Proceedings of the Royal Society of Medicine* (Epidemiology Section) 12 (1-2) (1919), pp. 77-120, and Matthew Young, 'An investigation into the periodicity of epidemics of whooping-cough from 1870-1910 by means of the periodogram', *Proceedings of the Royal Society of Medicine* (Epidemiology Section) 13 (1-2) (1920), pp. 207-236. They show that in Birmingham 1870-1910 the precise periodicity was 99 weeks for both diseases.

[49] Andrew D. Cliff, Peter Haggett and Matthew Smallman-Raynor, *Measles: An Historical Geography of a Major Human Viral Disease from Global Expansion to Local Retreat, 1840-1980* (Oxford: Blackwell, 1993), especially Chapter 4.

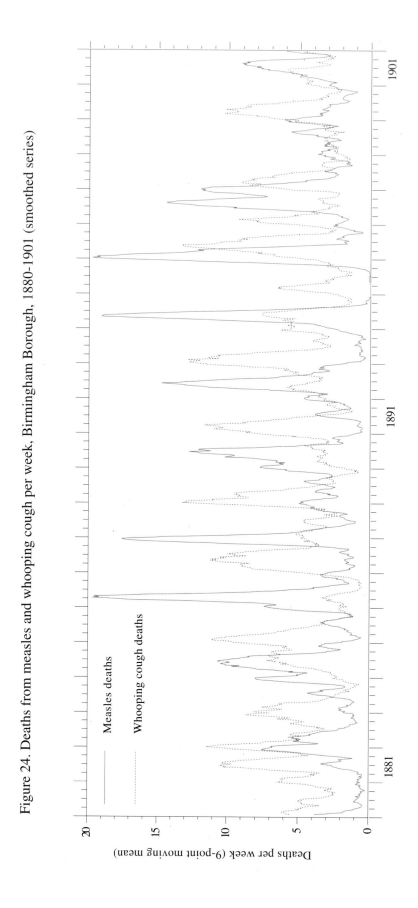

Figure 24. Deaths from measles and whooping cough per week, Birmingham Borough, 1880-1901 (smoothed series)

Figure 25. Relationship between Measles early childhood
mortality rate and population density, England and Wales,
1861-1870 and 1891-1900

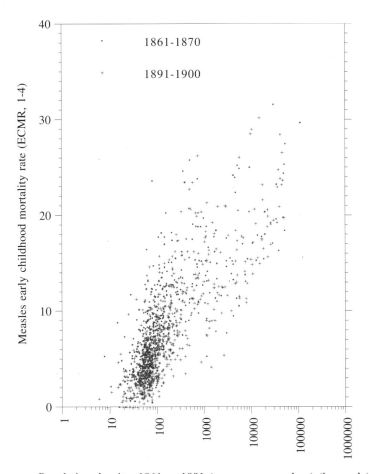

Population density, 1861 or 1891 (persons per sq. km.) (log scale)

Whooping cough early childhood mortality is shown in Map 15. Compared with Measles
the distribution of mortality from Whooping cough is not easy to account for. Although
some of the major towns are picked out, London included, there are also some highly
random elements which might be associated with any infectious disease. Mid-Wales in the
1860s and north Devon in the 1890s are good examples. Anne Hardy's *Epidemic Streets*
emphasises the point that whooping cough was to a large extent the poor relation of
childhood diseases: 'Declining death-rates from whooping cough were certainly not the
result of any direct intervention by the medical profession or preventive authorities, for
the disease aroused little interest among nineteenth-century practitioners and
epidemiologists' (p. 22). In this respect Map 15 does not really assist in bringing its
incidence more clearly into view, rather it may help us to appreciate the reasons for its
obscurity among contemporaries. The disease was of course an important killer in its own
right, but its links with measles also seem to have been important. Both diseases were
endemic with two to five year epidemic cycles in the large towns and simply epidemic

79

Map 14a. Measles early childhood mortality rate ages 1 – 4, England and Wales

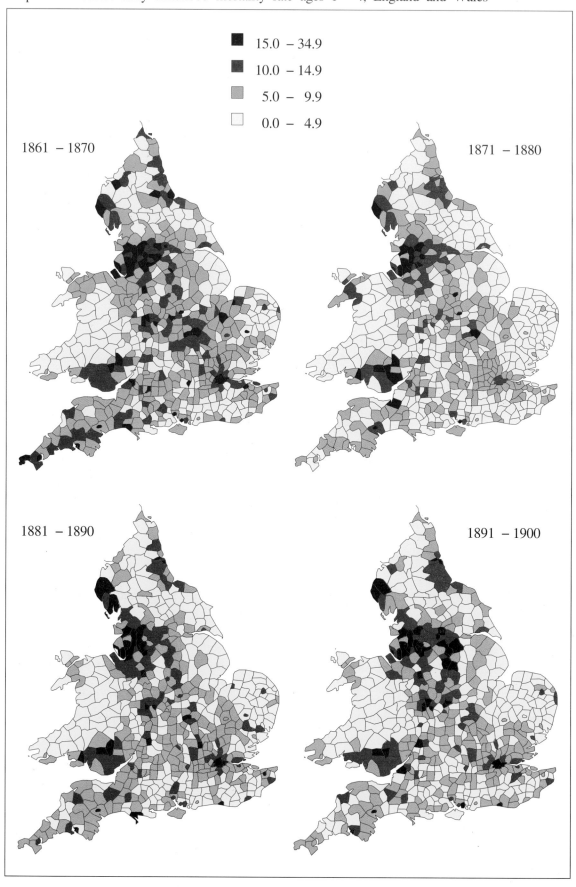

15.0 – 34.9
10.0 – 14.9
5.0 – 9.9
0.0 – 4.9

1861 – 1870

1871 – 1880

1881 – 1890

1891 – 1900

Map 14b. Measles early childhood mortality rate ages 1 – 4, London

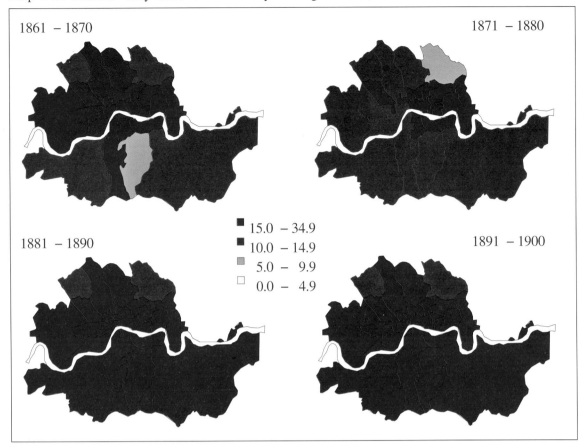

1861 – 1870

1871 – 1880

■ 15.0 – 34.9
■ 10.0 – 14.9
▨ 5.0 – 9.9
□ 0.0 – 4.9

1881 – 1890

1891 – 1900

Map 15. Whooping cough early childhood mortality rate ages 1 – 4

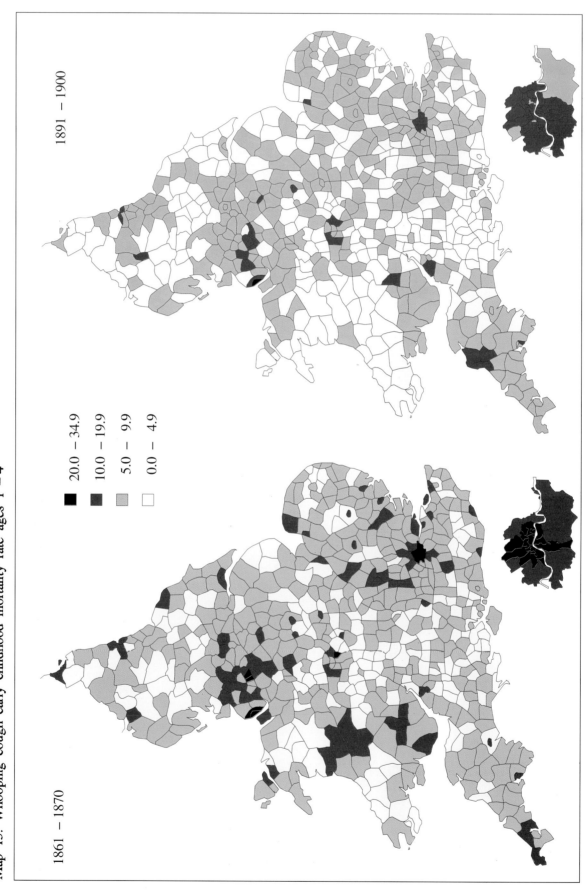

1861 – 1870

1891 – 1900

■ 20.0 – 34.9
■ 10.0 – 19.9
▨ 5.0 – 9.9
☐ 0.0 – 4.9

elsewhere. But contemporaries, including Charles Creighton, noticed that an epidemic of one often followed that of the other usually, he thought, in the sequence measles then whooping cough, but Brownlee and Young could not identify such a clear-cut sequence.[50] Either way, children born in the Victorian cities would have to face epidemics of summer diarrhoea in their first year, measles in their second and whooping cough in their third, each disease coming with complications and attendant dangers normally greater than the diseases themselves. The Aberdeen studies confirm the importance of secondary respiratory infections, especially bronchitis and pneumonia, associated with measles and diarrhoea linked with whooping cough, for example. Even those children who survived may have suffered lasting ill-effects in the form of susceptibility to tuberculosis and general weakness of the respiratory system.[51]

Measles and whooping cough are therefore especially interesting diseases in terms of their complementarity; their periodicity and focus on particular forms of densely populated urban environments, at least in the case of measles, and their failure to change radically before the twentieth century. The cases of scarlet fever and diphtheria are rather different. Childhood mortality from Scarlet fever, as Figures 6 and 22 illustrate, declined dramatically between the 1860s and 1890s while mortality from Diphtheria may have increased to some small degree. In this respect scarlet fever is one of the most interesting of infectious diseases to afflict Victorian children.

Figure 26 shows that neither scarlet fever nor diphtheria exhibited strong seasonality nor were they markedly periodic or epidemic in nature, although in the late 1880s and 1890s scarlet fever does appear to have had a return time after four years. Of the 22 years shown, roughly half experienced very few deaths from either cause. Figure 26 should be compared with Figure 24 in these respects. The relationship between Scarlet fever early childhood mortality and population density is shown for the 1860s and 1890s in Figure 27; again comparison with Measles in Figure 25 is useful. In the 1860s Scarlet fever mortality picks out some of the largest urban centres and it is certainly those places that benefit most from the lower mortality at the end of the century. This is also reflected in Maps 16a and 16b. But unlike Measles there are many counter-examples especially at mid-century of relatively high mortality in more rural areas. What is of most importance in terms of the disease's demographic impact is best illustrated by London which moves from black to red to orange to yellow shading through the four decades. By the 1890s Scarlet fever deaths had all but disappeared from most of South East England.

---

[50] Charles Creighton, *A History of Epidemics in Britain, Volume Two, From the Extinction of the Plague to the Present Time* (Cambridge: Cambridge University Press, 1894), p. 674; Hardy, *Epidemic Streets*, p. 21: 'Where poorly nourished children suffer an attack of measles, which further reduces nutritional status, followed within a few months by one of whooping cough, their chances of succumbing to the latter are greatly increased.' Brownlee, 'Epidemics of measles' and Young, 'Epidemics of whooping-cough', p. 230.

[51] West, *Lectures*, p. 854, Wilson, 'Measles', p. 76, and on the effects of the foetal and early childhood environment on adult health risks, see, David J. P. Barker, *Mothers, Babies, and Diseases in Later Life* (London: BMJ Publishing Group, 1994). This theme is taken up in Chapter 8 and especially Figure 38.

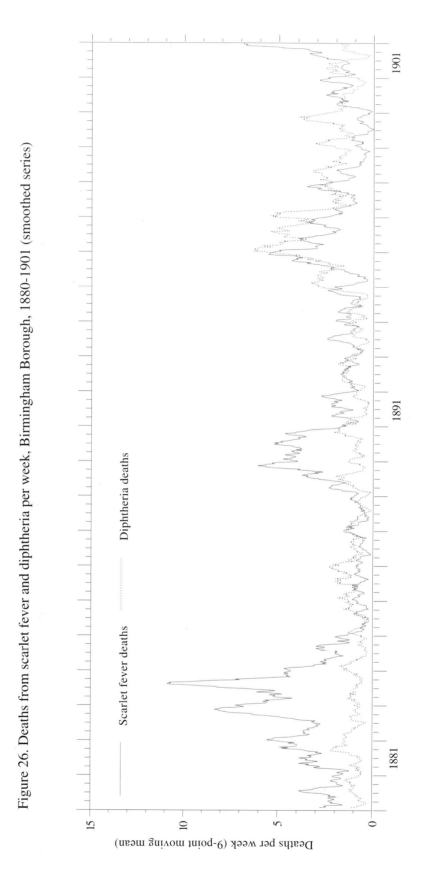

Figure 26. Deaths from scarlet fever and diphtheria per week, Birmingham Borough, 1880-1901 (smoothed series)

Map 16a. Scarlet fever early childhood mortality rate ages 1 −4, England and Wales

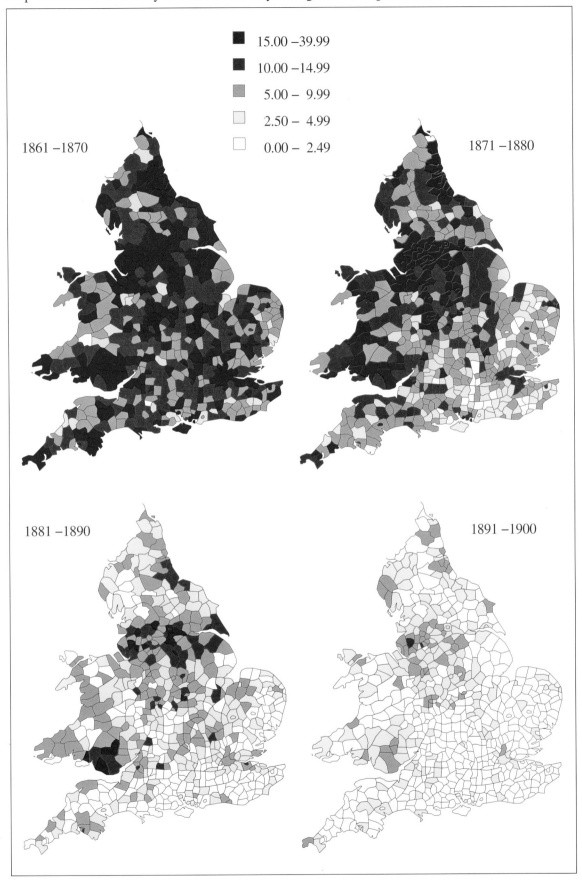

15.00 −39.99
10.00 −14.99
5.00 − 9.99
2.50 − 4.99
0.00 − 2.49

1861 −1870

1871 −1880

1881 −1890

1891 −1900

Map 16b. Scarlet fever early child mortality rate ages 1 –4, London

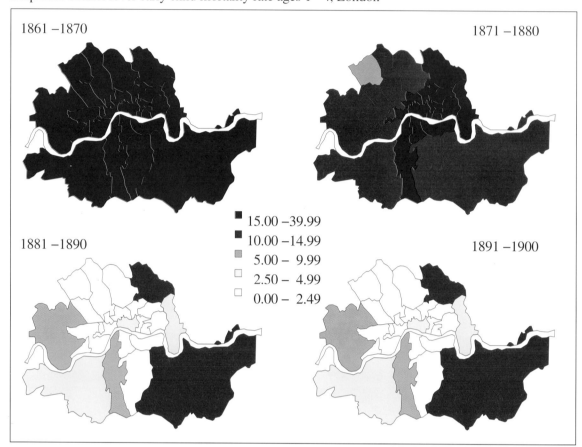

Map 17. Diphtheria early childhood mortality rate ages 1 – 4

1861 – 1870

1891 – 1900

10.0 – 54.9
5.0 – 9.9
2.5 – 4.9
0.0 – 2.4

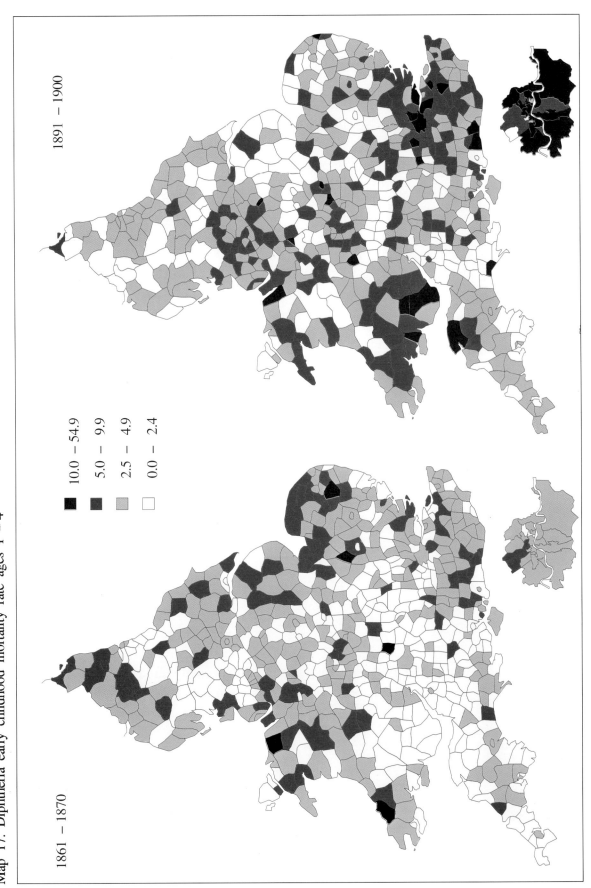

Figure 27. Relationship between Scarlet fever
early childhood mortality rate and population density,
England and Wales, 1861-1870 and 1891-1900

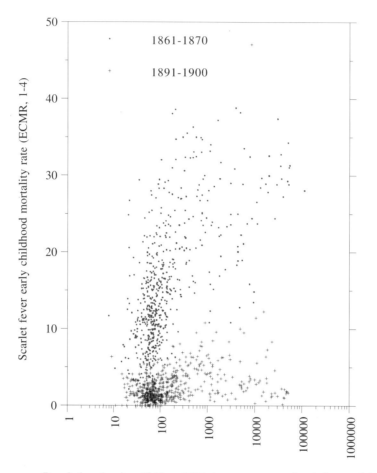

Population density, 1861 or 1891 (persons per sq. km.) (log scale)

By contrast Map 17 for Diphtheria early childhood mortality shows that in much of the South East and especially the area into which London was expanding as well as London itself, mortality from the disease had increased by the 1890s (see also Figure 7).[52] Although this phenomenon was not repeated in the other great towns of the Midlands and North. It has been suggested that to some extent diphtheria took scarlet fever's place, but if it did this certainly did not occur in most of England and Wales, and certainly not in the provincial towns.[53]

[52] Note that in Map 17 for London 1891-1900 the rate for Hampstead has not been shown (it was 94.5).

[53] See Arthur Newsholme, *Epidemic Diphtheria: A Research on the Origin and Spread of the Disease from an International Standpoint* (London: Swan Sonnenschein, 1898), and Marie C. Nelson, 'Diphtheria in late-nineteenth-century Sweden: policy and practice', *Continuity and Change* 9 (1994), pp. 213-242 provides a detailed recent study for Sweden.

88

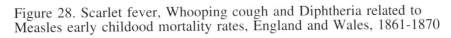

Figure 28. Scarlet fever, Whooping cough and Diphtheria related to
Measles early childood mortality rates, England and Wales, 1861-1870

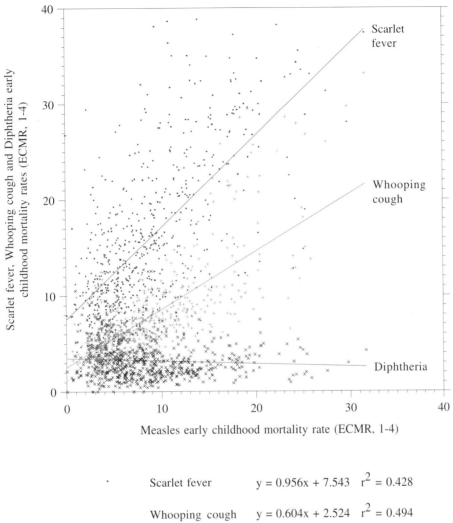

Scarlet fever	$y = 0.956x + 7.543$	$r^2 = 0.428$
Whooping cough	$y = 0.604x + 2.524$	$r^2 = 0.494$
Diphtheria	$y = -0.028x + 3.447$	$r^2 = 0.006$

One of the most intriguing aspects of childhood epidemiology is the extent to which the common diseases coincide in terms of the populations they most affect.[54] To some extent this can be illustrated by comparing the maps in Chapter 6, but it may also be helpful to consider mortality rates directly, at least for the 1860s. This is done in Figure 28 using Measles ECMR as the standard against which to compare geographical variations in Scarlet fever, Whooping cough and Diphtheria. As one would expect from what has gone before, Whooping cough and Measles are the pair most closely associated followed by Scarlet fever. Variations in Diphtheria are not statistically associated with any of the other three diseases. The *alpha* and *beta* coefficients in the regression equations indicate

---

[54] The concept of 'insult accumulation' is an important one that has largely been ignored in historical epidemiological studies which tend to consider single diseases rather than the sequence that may affect especially young children.

Map 18. Diseases of the Lung (1860s) and Diseases of the Respiratory system (1890s) early childhood mortality rate ages 1 – 4

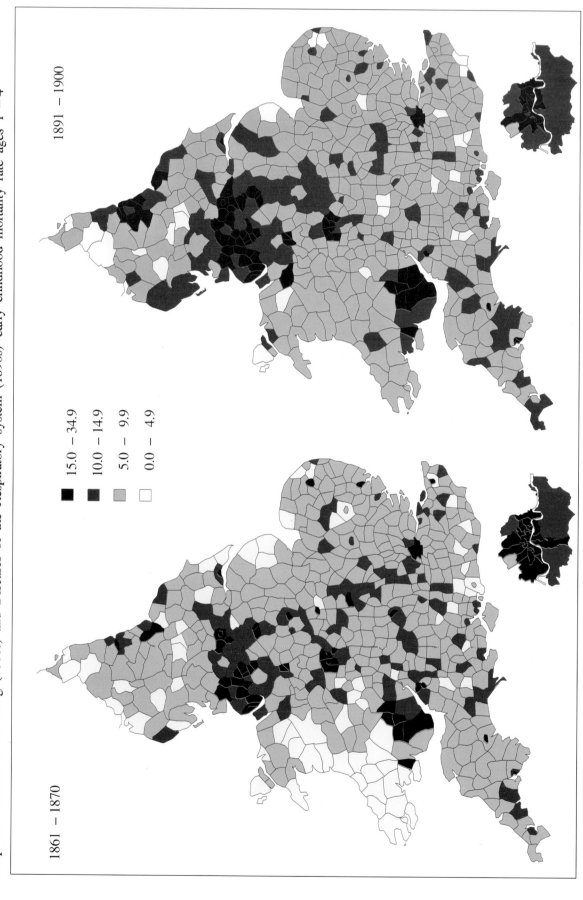

1891 – 1900

15.0 – 34.9
10.0 – 14.9
5.0 – 9.9
0.0 – 4.9

1861 – 1870

Map 19. Diseases of the Brain (1860s) and Diseases of the Nervous system (1890s) early childhood mortality rate ages 1 – 4

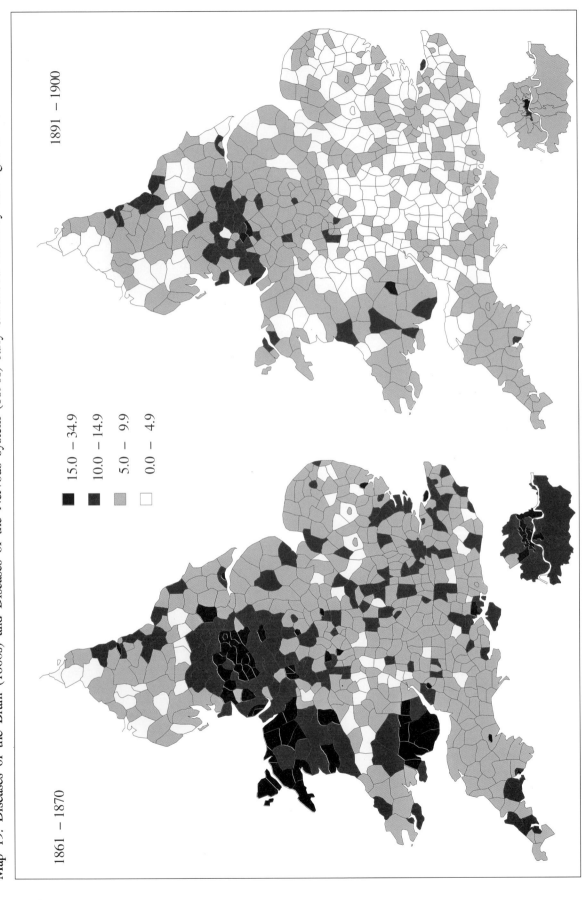

1861 – 1870

1891 – 1900

15.0 – 34.9
10.0 – 14.9
5.0 – 9.9
0.0 – 4.9

that ECMR from Scarlet fever was generally higher than that for Measles, while Whooping cough was higher in those districts where Measles was at its lowest, but rather more equal where Measles was at its highest. In combination these four diseases exerted a profound influence on childhood mortality, but especially that experienced in cities like Birmingham (see Figure 21).

To conclude this chapter on mortality in early childhood it is appropriate to reconsider Diseases of the Lung with Diseases of the Respiratory system and Diseases of the Brain with Diseases of the Nervous system. (Maps 18 and 19 should be compared with Maps 8 and 9 for infant mortality from the same causes.) As Figure 6 makes clear, the respiratory diseases held a particularly prominent place as killers of young children in Victorian England. If anything their position as the principal set of causes of death was enhanced by the 1890s. But as one would expect their impact was far from geographically uniform. Lung and Respiratory diseases were especially important in London, South Wales, the Black Country and Birmingham, the towns of Lancashire and the West Riding of Yorkshire, and County Durham. Districts like Wrexham and Stoke on Trent also stand out quite distinctly (Map 18). As far as Diseases of the Brain and Diseases of the Nervous system are concerned, North and South Wales stand out quite prominently in Map 19 just as they did in Map 10, but in the North of England the high childhood mortality rates are experienced by rather fewer and distinctly urban districts compared with the levels of mortality from these diseases in infancy which cover a far wider area of the North.

Mortality in early childhood beyond infancy is one of the most important, complicated, interesting and yet neglected aspects of the epidemiology of Victorian England. Important because childhood mortality (at least ages 2-14) did decline and thereby had a bearing on the improvement in life expectancy at birth. Complicated because some of the common diseases of childhood probably attacked their victims in sequence so that the cumulative effects were at least additive if not multiplicative. Some of these diseases were also highly sensitive to the effects of crowding accentuated by population growth and urbanisation, perhaps even more so that the water-borne diseases at which the sanitary revolution was targeted. Interesting because so many questions remain unanswered about the incidence of such diseases as measles and whooping cough, about the causes of the decline of scarlet fever mortality, and the effects of childhood morbidity on life chances in adulthood especially the consequences for tuberculosis and the respiratory diseases in general.

7

Young adults

The most intriguing feature of the mortality curve for young adults—those aged 10 to 34—is the phenomenon known as the 'trauma hump'.[55] Today this hump is associated mostly with deaths due to accidents, but in the nineteenth century other influences also made important contributions. Figure 29 uses English Life Tables 3 and 6 for 1838-1854 and 1891-1900 to illustrate the location of the hump and how it diminished during the Victorian period (see also Figure 2). At mid-century there was a distinctive kink in the probability of dying by single years of age curve at age 20, but by the end of the century not only had mortality at each age 5-40 declined, but the kink in the curve seems to have largely disappeared.

When one compares females with males, what Farr defined as healthy districts with all districts, then the simple outline given by Figure 29 begins to blur. Figure 30 shows curves for males and females as well as distinguishing between the two sets of districts. The issue of gender differentials in mortality will be returned to in Chapter 12 although it may be noted here in passing that it is in the young adult ages that excess female mortality is most likely to be experienced in the nineteenth century, and certainly in the early decades of civil registration to which English Life Table 3 applies. But Figure 30 also shows that the mortality hump was equally present and coincidental in terms of age in the curves for both males and females, all and not just healthy districts at mid-century. Although by the 1890s there is still a recognisable hump in the mortality curves for females, it is far more muted and comes at an earlier age, 17 instead of 20. For males the hump is even less obvious and for the healthy districts it comes at 22.

Figures 29 and 30 help to further emphasise the point that the Victorian experience of mortality decline was highly focused in terms of age and that most occurred as the result of improvements in the life chances of children and young adults. But they also demonstrate once again that the structure of mortality changed and that this was the direct consequence of one or a number of shifts in the dominant cause of death pattern. Even a casual glance at Figure 6 will reveal that mortality among young adults was dominated by Phthisis or pulmonary tuberculosis. Indeed, tuberculosis was so important for this age group and for the larger story of mortality change and variation in Victorian England and Wales that it must merit a chapter on its own. It will also be obvious that maternal

[55] James C. Riley, 'Excess mortality in youth', in David S. Reher and Roger Schofield (eds.) *Old and New Methods in Historical Demography* (Oxford: Clarendon Press, 1993), pp. 394-409.

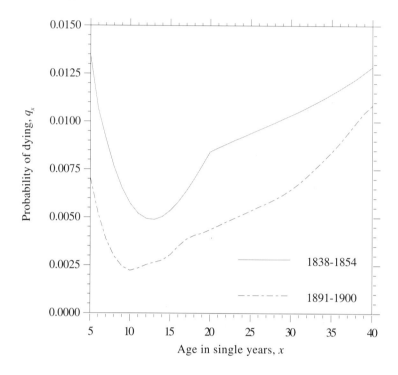

Figure 29. Probabilities of dying by single years of age between 5 and 40 from English Life Tables 3 & 6, England and Wales

mortality will have had a considerable influence on the age profile for females and that this too should merit separate consideration in its own chapter.

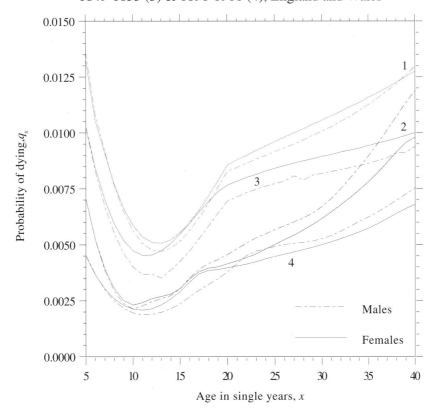

Figure 30. Probabilities of dying by single years of age between 5 and 40, males and females compared from English Life Tables 3 for 1838-1854 (1) & 6 for 1891-1900 (2) and Healthy Districts Life Tables for 1849-1853 (3) & 1891-1900 (4), England and Wales

8

Tuberculosis

There can be no doubt that pulmonary tuberculosis was one of the most important diseases in the nineteenth century both in terms of its changing demographic impact and the effect that such a debilitating disease could have on the health of the nation and the everyday lives of its people.[56] Here we are obliged to focus exclusively on Phthisis which is normally equated with the pulmonary form of tuberculosis (Table 2), although the new nosology applied in the first decade of the twentieth century distinguished a number of different forms of tuberculosis only one appears consistently in the *Decennial Supplements* which report mortality by districts. Pulmonary tuberculosis is a particularly complicated disease to deal with in epidemiological and demographic terms. Certainly the disease displayed age and gender biases which were modified as mortality declined during the second half of the nineteenth century. But it has also been suggested that the decline of phthisis was to some extent offset by the increase in deaths ascribed to respiratory diseases in general. Further, there is uncertainty concerning the extent to which pulmonary tuberculosis was principally an urban disease and whether the decline in mortality with which it was associated was ubiquitous and, if so, what this might imply.

The changing age and sex structure of Phthisis mortality has often been commented on and is illustrated again here in Figure 31.[57] While between the 1850s and the 1900s mortality from Phthisis declined at every age, it did so more for females than for males, but the shape of the mortality curves also changed so that the rapid increase between ages 10 and 20 so evident at mid-century and partly responsible for the characteristic kink shown in Figure 29 became far more muted by the first decade of the twentieth century. This chapter will focus, therefore, on the age groups 20-24 and 25-34 and will wherever possible distinguish between the experiences of males and females although unfortunately

---

[56] John Brownlee, *An Investigation into the Epidemiology of Phthisis in Great Britain and Ireland, Parts I, II and III*, Medical Research Council, Special Reports Nos. 18 and 46 (London: HMSO, 1918 and 1922) provides an early twentieth-century summary of the medical statistics while George Gregory Kayne, Water Pagel and Laurence O'Shaughnessy, *Pulmonary Tuberculosis: Pathology, Diagnosis, Management and Prevention* (Oxford: Oxford University Press, 1939) gives a medical survey and F. B. Smith, *The Retreat of Tuberculosis, 1850-1950* (London: Croom Helm, 1988) gives the medical historian's interpretation and Leonard G Wilson, 'The historical decline of tuberculosis in Europe and America: its causes and significance', *Journal of the History of Medicine* 45 (1990), pp. 49-57 offers a recent review and, Ian Sutherland, 'Recent studies in the epidemiology of tuberculosis', *Advances in Tuberculosis Research* 19 (1976), pp. 1-63 summarises recent epidemiological work. Hardy, *Epidemic Streets*, Chapter 8, 'Tuberculosis', and Linda Bryder, *Below the Magic Mountain: A Social History of Tuberculosis in the Twentieth Century* (Oxford: Clarendon Press, 1988) provide excellent introductions.

[57] Pierre-Charles-Alexandre Louis, 'Note sur la fréquence relative de la phthisie chez les deux sexes', *Annales d'Hygiène Publique* 6 (1831), pp. 49-57 was one of the first to document the differential using clinical evidence.

Figure 31. Age-specific mortality rates from Phthisis
for men and women, England and Wales,
1851-1860 to 1901-1910 (six decades)
(Note: the curves for men 1851-1860 and 1901-1910
are also shown on the graph for women.)

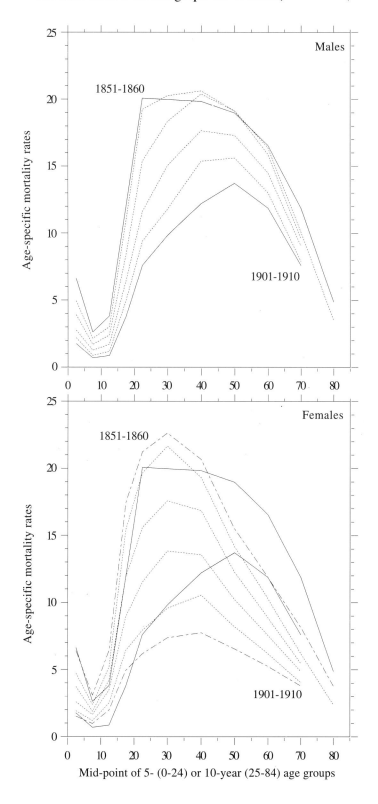

Mid-point of 5- (0-24) or 10-year (25-84) age groups

97

this will not be possible for the 1870s, 1880s and 1890s. In general it would appear that Phthisis mortality not only declined, but that there may also have been an element of postponement. Certainly the mortality rate among young adults was much reduced although this should not lead us to conclude that a lower proportion of Victorian twenty year olds had contracted tuberculosis, simply that it had not yet proved fatal. The effects of 'galloping consumption' became less important, perhaps.

Since phthisis attacked the lung it might seem reasonable to classify it as one of the Diseases of the Lung or Diseases of the Respiratory system and this probably did happen especially when the immediate cause of death was pneumonia or bronchitis, and particularly in old age. But the symptoms of pulmonary tuberculosis were quite distinctive as a chronic disease, its age profile was characteristic, as was also its lack of seasonality.[58] Figure 32 shows what could be expected in a city like Birmingham. Deaths from respiratory diseases follow a strong pattern of seasonal variation while those from phthisis display far less seasonality, although there is some first quarter excess. Phthisis is not a dramatic disease, rather it is insidious in its debilitating effects and inexorable in its ultimate consequence. Its weekly death toll displays a monotonous regularity.

'The theory that urban areas in particular fostered tuberculosis, and that rural life afforded some protection against the disease, was an important part of nineteenth-century explanations of regional variations in the rates.'[59] Such an interpretation would be far too simple, however. Figure 33 shows the relationship between Phthisis mortality rates for 20-24 year olds against population density for the 614 districts. Clearly, some of the very highest Phthisis rates are in rural districts, but then so are the very lowest rates. The large urban centres experience only average rates. Unlike infant Diarrhoea & Dysentery and certainly childhood Measles there was no neatly defined association between Phthisis mortality in early adulthood and whether a place was urban or rural. Maps 20a, 20b, 21a and 21b help to make the point forcefully.[60] In the 1860s there were groups of districts in East Anglia, the north Pennines and especially west Wales in which Phthisis was particularly high, these were also some of the most rural of areas. It is also the case that none of the urban-industrial areas which we have come to associate with high mortality from virtually every individual cause of death were prominent where Phthisis in early adulthood is concerned.

---

[58] See Hardy, *Epidemic Streets*, pp. 215-218 and 229-230, but also Bryder, 'Not always', on the problems of using tuberculosis statistics. Farr, *Vital Statistics*, pp. 266-269, attempted a comparison of phthisis and bronchitis mortality by age for 1848-1863, but this was largely inconclusive as to the problems of registration. Farr's first wife died from consumption in her early twenties.

[59] Gillian Cronjé, 'Tuberculosis and mortality decline in England and Wales, 1851-1910', in Robert Woods and John Woodward (eds.), *Urban Disease and Mortality in Nineteenth-Century England* (London: Batsford, 1984), p. 93. Using the 45 registration counties, Cronjé concludes that, 'The statistical data thus bear out the contemporary belief that rural areas escaped more lightly from tuberculosis than urban counties' (p. 94).

[60] It should be remembered that the presence of hospitals like the Brompton in Kensington which specialised in tuberculosis cases is likely to distort Phthisis mortality patterns among the London districts.

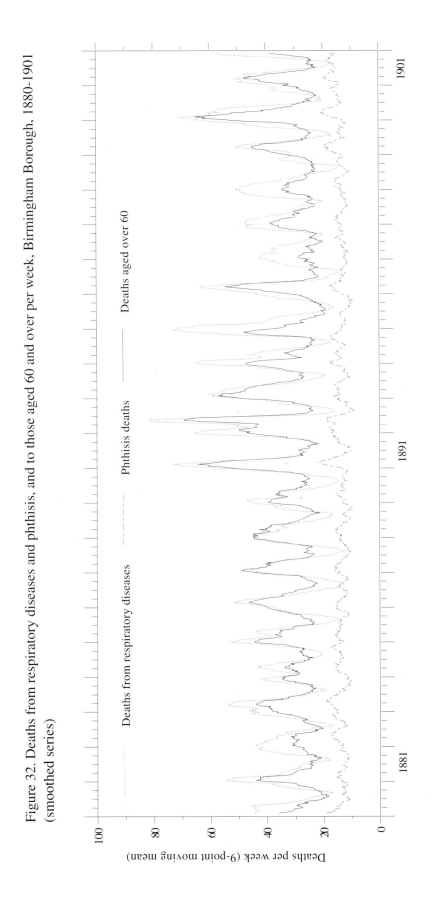

Figure 32. Deaths from respiratory diseases and phthisis, and to those aged 60 and over per week, Birmingham Borough, 1880-1901 (smoothed series)

Deaths from respiratory diseases   Phthisis deaths   Deaths aged over 60

Deaths per week (9-point moving mean)

100   80   60   40   20   0

1881   1891   1901

99

Map 20a. Phthisis mortality rate ages 20 – 24, England and Wales

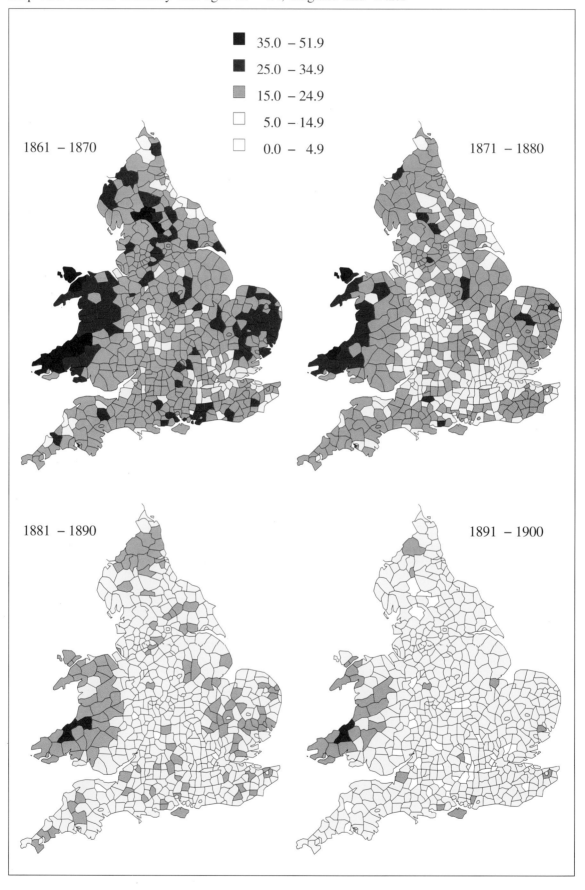

Map 20b. Phthisis mortality rate ages 20 – 24, London

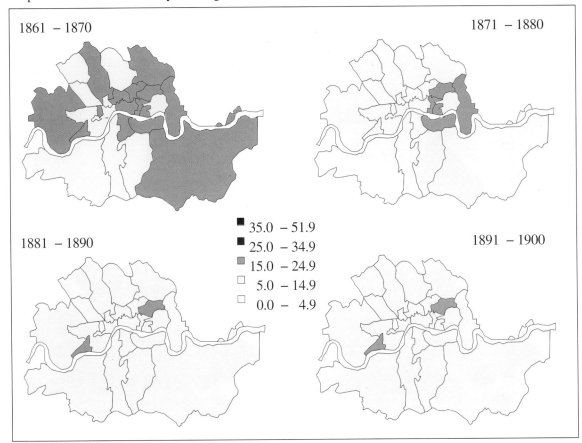

1861 – 1870

1871 – 1880

■ 35.0 – 51.9
■ 25.0 – 34.9
▨ 15.0 – 24.9
□ 5.0 – 14.9
□ 0.0 – 4.9

1881 – 1890

1891 – 1900

Map 21a. Phthisis mortality rate ages 25 – 34, England and Wales

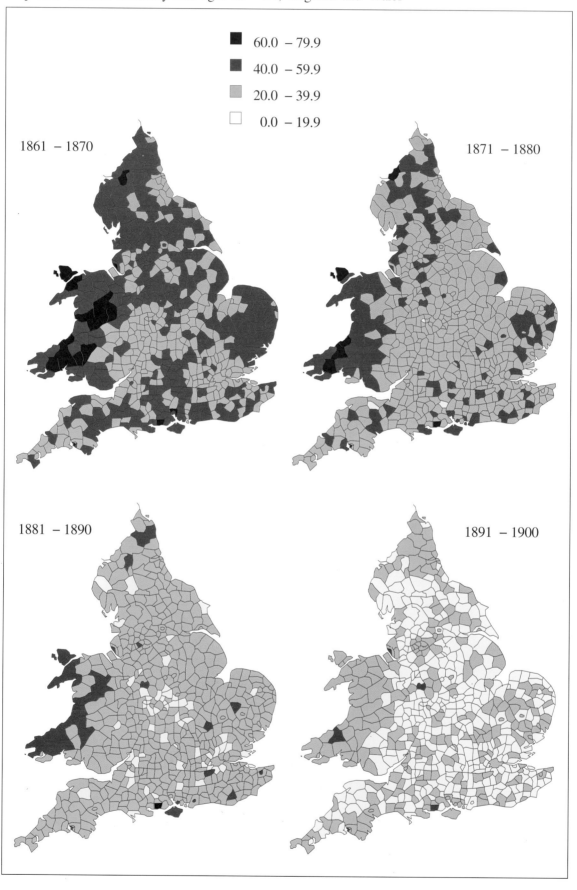

60.0 – 79.9
40.0 – 59.9
20.0 – 39.9
0.0 – 19.9

1861 – 1870

1871 – 1880

1881 – 1890

1891 – 1900

Map 21b. Phthisis mortality rate ages 25 – 34, London

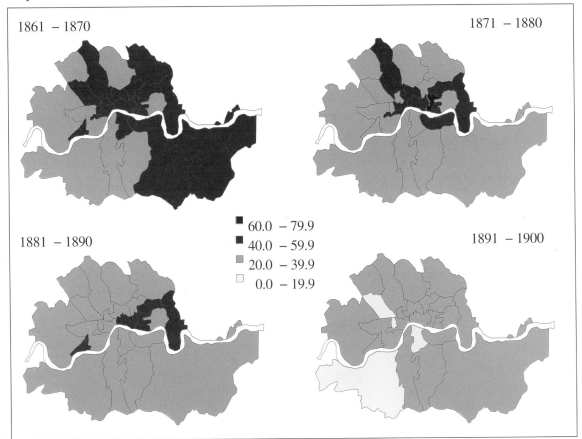

Figure 33. Relationship between Phthisis
early adult mortality rate and population density,
England and Wales, 1861-1870 and 1891-1900

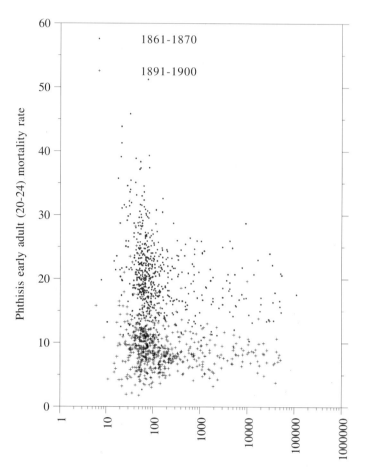

Population density, 1861 or 1891 (persons per sq. km.) (log scale)

Of course, what is most interesting about Figure 33 and Maps 20 and 21 is that Phthisis mortality appears to have declined in nearly all districts regardless of initial rate or whether the place had urban or rural characteristics. However, it is not a straightforward matter to capture the dimensions of these changes. For example, Figure 34 shows Phthisis mortality rates in the 1890s against those for the 1860s. There is a significant positive association in the cases of 20-24 and 25-34, and the *beta* coefficient is also substantially less than one, but the experience of the two age groups whilst similar cannot be said to be equal.

Figure 35 makes an attempt to compare relative percentage change in the age groups. All districts in the 0-100 space experienced decline at both 20-24 and 25-34 while those places in the 50-100 space had mortality more than halve in both age groups. However, some of the more interesting cases are to be found among those districts in which 20-24 mortality declined by more than a half but that for the 25-34 age group fell by less than a half (3), and the group of districts in which decline in 25-34 was in excess of 20-24 (2).

Figure 34. Phthisis mortality rates for age groups
20-24 and 25-34, 1891-1900 against 1861-1870,
England and Wales

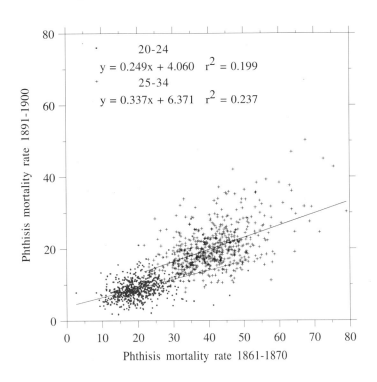

Figure 35. Association between relative percentage
decline 1861-1870 to 1891-1900 of Phthisis mortality
rates for age group 25-34 against 20-24, England and Wales

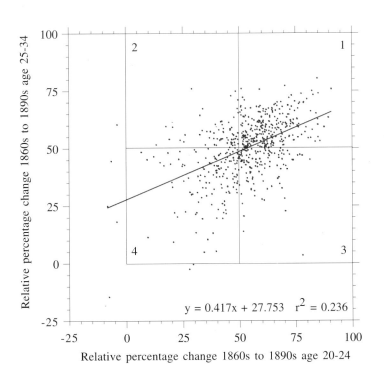

Map 22. Categories of relative change in Phthisis mortality from Figure 35

These districts, together with those in the other two quarters of Figure 35 (1 and 4), are shown on Map 22. There are many districts in England where Phthisis mortality in both age groups more than halved between the 1860s and the 1890s (1 in Map 22) and these are widespread in parts of the rural North, the south Midlands and East Anglia. But there are also many districts in the North East and the South West of both England and Wales where although there was decline at both 20-24 and 25-34 the relative change in both age groups was far less strong (4). In North Wales and a scattering of other districts including several in London, Phthisis mortality in the age group 20-24 declined faster than at 25-34 (3); and in some districts (mid-Devon and mid-Kent provide examples of clusters) mortality at the older age group declined faster than at the younger (2). The patterns illustrated by Figure 35 and Map 22 are not easy to interpret, but there is evidence that clusters of districts existed which experienced similar sorts of patterns of change and that in some of those clusters Phthisis mortality was rather slow to decline at all young adult ages (4). These districts were not all rural or urban, rather there were examples of each, but they do show some signs of sub-regional clustering consistent with the maintenance of higher levels of infection among certain geographically distinctive populations.

Since we are not able to distinguish among districts between the Phthisis mortality of males and females from the 1870s to the 1890s, it will not be possible to trace the geographical manifestations of the age and gender shifts in the mortality curve which have been illustrated in Figure 31. But we are able to explore the relationship between the Phthisis mortality of males and females at least for the 1860s. This is shown in ratio form in Figure 36 where it is plotted against population density, and in Map 23. While it can be concluded that excess female mortality from Phthisis in the 20-24 age group was experienced mainly in rural districts (curves labelled 3 in Figure 30) and that the largest urban centres tended to have excess male mortality, some rural districts experienced exceptionally high excess male mortality. Map 23 also picks these districts out.

Victorian reports on phthisis regularly mentioned the link between maternal deaths and the incidence of tuberculosis, but since the 1930s these simple connections have been challenged. It now seems more likely that the exertions of labour may have accelerated the development of tuberculous lesions in the lungs of those females already infected.[61] Repeated pregnancies may have increased the phthisis mortality rate among already infected females—the presence of such infection would certainly have reduced the life chances of their children—but the chances of dying during or shortly after pregnancy are influenced by many other factors apart from pulmonary tuberculosis (see Chapter 9). The lack of relationship shown by the scatter of points in Figure 37 should not be a surprise, therefore.

---

[61] Kayne et al., *Pulmonary Tuberculosis*, pp. 168-169.

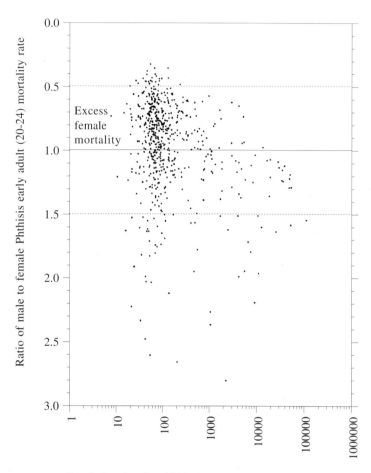

Figure 36. Ratio of male to female Phthisis
early adult mortality rate against population density,
England and Wales, 1861-1870

Population density, 1861 (persons per sq. km.) (log scale)

Also current in the nineteenth century was the idea that children weakened by measles or whooping cough at an early age, or prone to the respiratory diseases would be more likely to succumb to phthisis in adulthood, assuming survival beyond childhood.[62] Whilst this is not implausible, it is more likely that infants and young children infected with the tubercle bacillus would after reinfection in their teens become victims of the disease in their twenties or thirties. These forms of age and cohort relationships are particularly difficult to demonstrate even with the longitudinal data sets available in the twentieth century, and the civil registration system of the last century offers very few opportunities. One approach is attempted in Figure 38. It represents the association among districts of early childhood mortality from respectively Phthisis and Diseases of the Lung in the 1860s with variations in early adulthood mortality from Phthisis twenty years on. In neither case can it be said that there is strong evidence for a conditioning relationship; just because mortality from Phthisis or Diseases of the Lung was high among children the

[62] The influence of foetal and early childhood environments on adult health has recently become a subject for discussion and research effort. See David J. P. Barker, 'Rise and fall of Western diseases', *Nature* 338 (1989), pp. 371-372, and especially *Mothers, Babies, and Diseases in Later Life.*

Map 23. Ratio of male to female Phthisis mortality ages 20 – 24, 1861 – 1870

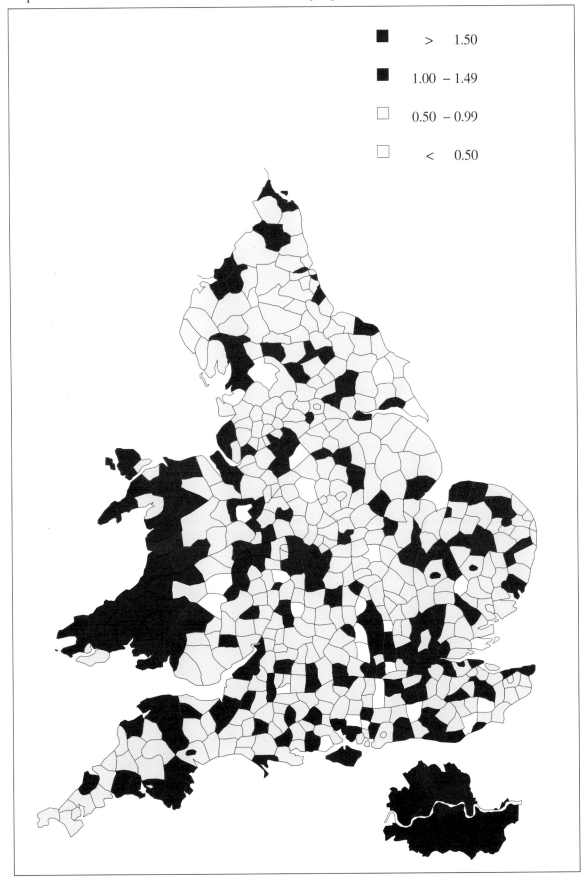

Figure 37. Relationship between Phthisis mortality
in women and maternal mortality, England and Wales

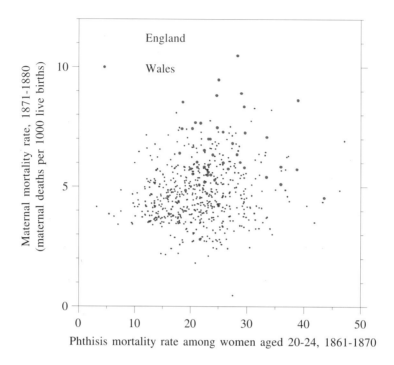

Phthisis mortality rate among women aged 20-24, 1861-1870

ecological evidence gives no support to the claim that this is likely to mean that those who reached adulthood would succumb to high rates of Phthisis mortality. Indeed, Figure 38 shows that if there is a link between Diseases of the Lung in childhood and subsequent Phthisis mortality among the populations of districts then it is more likely to be a negative one. Figure 38 distinguishes between the English and Welsh districts because, as we have seen, young adult mortality from Phthisis was especially prominent among males and was particularly high in certain Welsh districts although like Diseases of the Lung it does not appear to have been high in early childhood.

While he was Medical Officer of Health for Brighton Arthur Newsholme prepared a lengthy report on the decline in the phthisis death rate.[63] He concludes as follows.

> 'Segregation in general institutions is the only factor which has varied constantly with the phthisis death-rate in the countries that have been examined. It must therefore be regarded as having exerted a more powerful influence on the

[63] Arthur Newsholme, 'An inquiry into the principal causes of the reduction in death-rate from phthisis during the last forty years, with special reference to the segregation of phthisical patients in general institutions', *Journal of Hygiene* 6 (1906), pp. 304-384. This is a substantial study which exemplifies Newsholme's method. Although the importance attached in its conclusion to the significance of one factor is probably unjustified, the assessment of the relative contributions of other factors is more convincing.

Figure 38. Relationships between Phthsis mortality rate 20-24 in 1881-1890 and Phthisis and Diseases of the Lung ECMR (1-4) 1861-1870, England and Wales

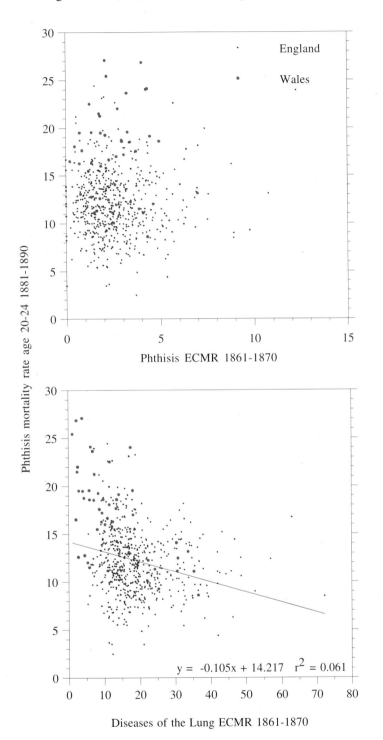

111

prevention of phthisis than any of the other factors of which none has varied constantly with the phthisis death-rate.'[64]

The other factors to which Newsholme refers are: urbanisation and industrialisation; 'improved housing and decreased overcrowding', ('Overcrowding is an important factor of the phthisis-rate but its effect is usually not strong enough to counteract the influence of other factors.'); nutrition, ('The consumption of food per head shows no correspondence with the extent of prevalence of phthisis;...'); poverty, (pauperism is too heterogeneous a concept in itself, but some of its elements may have an important influence); improved knowledge of and education about phthisis, (post-dates a well-marked decrease in the disease); and the introduction of sanatoria, ('...insignificant in number relatively to the amount of the disease.').[65]

Newsholme's principal argument is that the increased treatment of phthisis cases in workhouses or workhouse infirmaries led to the removal of infection from the wider community. By the late 1890s and early 1900s up to a third of all phthisis deaths in London occurred in Poor Law institutions. In Sheffield and Salford the figure was closes to 25 per cent, in Brighton it was 20 per cent and in Newport (Monmouthshire) it was closer to 14 per cent.[66] While it is certainly the case that the percentage of all phthisis deaths occurring in institutions did increase during the last decades of the nineteenth century (from less that 15 per cent in the towns in the 1880s to from 20 to 30 per cent in the early 1900s) and this would certainly have helped to remove infectives from the community during the last stages of their illness, it is not clear whether these percentages are sufficiently high sufficiently early in the nineteenth century to have made an initial impact on the downward trend of phthisis mortality. It is also unclear from the evidence Newsholme presents whether the phthisis deaths in institutions fell into any particular age groups, the aged poor for example. If they did, then the strength of his case would be much weakened since, as we have seen in Figure 31, much of the reduction in phthisis mortality came between ages 15 and 50.

There are still many aspects of the historical epidemiology of pulmonary tuberculosis which are not and probably cannot be understood. The factors that influenced the duration and intensity of exposure to infection or reinfection; that led to the active manifestation of the characteristic symptoms of phthisis, especially the spitting of foul mucoid sputum and haemoptysis; and the factors that finally led to death from the disease or where pulmonary tuberculosis was an important contributory complication, each need to be distinguished separately. While it is certain that mortality due to pulmonary tuberculosis did decline in the second half of the nineteenth century in England and

---

[64] Newsholme, 'An inquiry', p. 375. Some of Newsholme's ideas may have been influenced by Robert Koch's Nobel lecture of 1905. See Robert Koch, 'How the fight against tuberculosis now stands', *Lancet* 1 (4317) (1906), pp. 1449-1451.

[65] Newsholme, 'An inquiry', quoted from p. 374.

[66] Newsholme, 'An inquiry', p. 370.

Wales, that the age and gender profiles changed, and that this had a profound effect on death rates in general and the life chances of young adults in particular, it is still unclear what caused these changes.

The McKeown interpretation holds that the nutritional status of the population improved sufficiently to reduce the risk of dying from phthisis, the rate of infection did not decline and that therapy before the 1950s was largely ineffective.[67] Although McKeown had no direct evidence for the improvement of nutritional status, more recent work by Floud, Wachter and Gregory using time-series of average heights concludes that, 'the fall in mortality in late nineteenth-century England and Wales follows almost exactly the pattern we would expect from the evidence of nutritional status [from the 1860 birth cohort]. The height data make the link between nutrition (although in a wider sense) and mortality which McKeown could only infer' and, 'There is little doubt that the second half of the nineteenth century or more precisely the fifty-five years from 1860 to the outbreak of the First World War, saw significant improvements in the nutritional status of the British people and that these improvements were reflected in reductions in mortality and morbidity levels. The evidence of mean heights correlates so well with that of mortality that this inference is fully justified.'[68] F. B. Smith's conclusion is rather more circumspect, 'Better nutrition, housing, nurture, lessening of fatigue, smaller family size acting synergistically in varying permutations through time and place hold the answer, although that answer remains vague because its chronology and linkages are little traced or understood.'[69]

How does the evidence presented in this chapter relate to these arguments? To simplify, suppose we distinguish between the influence of nutrition and that of housing quality, and accept the need to account for both variations and changes in mortality attributed to phthisis. Maps 20 and 21 do not help us to form a judgement either one way or another, rather they encourage us to reflect on whether we are asking the right questions. Many of the districts with the highest levels of Phthisis mortality at both 20-24 and 25-34 are in the most remote rural areas little affected by in-migration although

[67] McKeown, *Modern Rise of Population*.

[68]Roderick Floud, Kenneth Wachter and Annabel Gregory, *Height, Health and History: Nutritional Status in the United Kingdom, 1750-1980* (Cambridge: Cambridge University Press, 1990), pp. 314 and 319. There has been a long and still active debate on the history of nutrition and the interpretation of height data. See, Robert W. Fogel, 'Economic growth, population theory, and physiology: the bearing of long-term processes on the making of economic policy', *American Economic Review* 84 (1994), pp. 369-395, and 'The relevance of Malthus for the study of mortality today: long-run influences on health, mortality, labour force participation, and population growth', in Kerstin Lindahl-Kiessling and Hans Landberg (eds.) *Population, Economic Development and the Environment* (Oxford: Oxford University Press, 1994), pp. 231-284. Fogel argues that 'when final heights are used to explain differences in adult mortality rates, they reveal the effect, not of adult levels of nutrition on adult mortality rates, but of nutritional levels during infancy, childhood, and adolescence on adult mortality rates.' (p. 243)

[69] Smith, *Retreat of Tuberculosis*, p. 244. See also, Hardy, *Epidemic Streets*, p. 213, 'The continuing challenge of historical tuberculosis research is to achieve a finer evaluation of the balance of factors driving the decline of the disease.'

experiencing depopulation.[70] Here mortality is high because infection and reinfection rates are high, and housing may be both poor and overcrowded. But in general these maps do not provide support for interpretations that emphasise either changes in nutritional status or the quality of housing or, indeed, some synergistic interaction between the two. Rather, they point towards closer scrutiny of either the nature of pulmonary tuberculosis itself and especially its virulence or the effects health-selective migration might have when such a chronic disease is involved or the manner of Phthisis death registration.

The simplest explanation is that the disease became less virulent and that this was the principal reason for a reduction in the risk of the disease developing and leading to early death, that this process occurred slowly and everywhere. This does not mean that registration fashion might not have had a bearing, but this is rather more likely in the early twentieth century when consumptives were liable to be put away in sanatoria and after the 1911 National Insurance Act which tended to discriminate against families with a known history of tuberculosis. Nor does it mean that poor nutrition, overcrowded housing and poverty in general did not influence the outcome and its speed once the disease began to develop, but it does mean that it is no longer necessary to search for substantial and widespread improvements in living standards in order to explain the decline of Phthisis mortality and thus the slow increase in adult life expectancy in the late nineteenth century. Persistent geographical differentiation in the quality of life should be mirrored by tuberculosis deaths, that it was not in this case should tell us more about epidemiology than economic and social history.[71]

---

[70] The possibility that selective out-migration of the healthy combined with low levels of in-migration may have affected the disease environments of some especially rural districts is taken up in Chapter 12, which considers gender differences in mortality, and migration trends are illustrated in Map 34. See Welton, 'Effects of migration', and Hardy, *Epidemic Streets*, pp. 250-253 with respect to London migrants.

[71] This re-emphasis on the disease itself rather than the conditions of vulnerability requires far greater attention than it has received in recent years. McKeown's often repeated assertion that, 'There is no evidence that the virulence of the organism has changed significantly; the disease continues to have devastating effects on populations not previously exposed to it; and the virulence of the bacillus appears not to have diminished during the period when it has been possible to assess it in the laboratory', (*Modern Rise of Population*, p. 83) will need to be countered first. Robert Koch, 'How the fight against tuberculosis now stands', is, of course, especially informative on the matter of infection. These dangers are at their greatest ' the more uncleanly the [already infected] patients are as regards their sputum, the more lack there is of light and air, and the more closely crowded together the sick live with the hale. The danger of infection becomes especially great when healthy people have to sleep in the same rooms with sick people and even, as unfortunately still frequently happens among the poor, in the same bed.' (p. 1449) Koch's lecture is a salutary reminder that even the poorest, most undernourished and badly housed would not die from tuberculosis if they were not first infected by a person with the disease. With notification, a degree of isolation especially of those in the last stages of the disease, and health education tuberculosis mortality could be reduced. (Koch regarded bovine tuberculosis as relatively unimportant.) While Koch's account helps to explain the existence of certain differentials in tuberculosis mortality as well as its accelerating decline after the 1880s, it does not help us understand the earlier phase of decline in countries like England and Wales.

9

Maternal mortality

Maternal deaths are usually defined in the following way: those deaths which occur in pregnancy, labour, or the post-natal period (taken to be 4 weeks in Victorian England) and which are due to obstetric causes only.[72] In terms of the *Decennial Supplements,* maternal deaths are given separately for the 1860s onwards which makes it possible to overcome the difficulty of using Childbirth and Metria for the 1850s and 1860s, and Puerperal fever and Childbirth in the following four decades (see Table 2). The reported number of maternal deaths may simply be expressed as a ratio per thousand live births in each district and it is this definition which is adopted here and shown in Maps 24a and 24b rather than relating Childbirth deaths to some estimate of the female population by age. Although the maternal mortality rate for England and Wales changed very little in the last half of the nineteenth century (it was 4.70 in the 1850s and 1860s; 4.75 1870s; 4.73 1880s; 5.09 1890s; decreased to 4.00 1900s; 4.07 in the 1910s and 1920s; and only in the mid-1930s began a precipitous decline) there were nonetheless some distinct local and regional variations.

'One of the most striking and least understood features of maternal mortality was the wide regional variations.'[73] Loudon's observation is still appropriate even when we deal with districts rather than counties or regional divisions. Map 24 shows that there are areas in which the maternal mortality rate is persistently higher than the level for England and Wales as a whole, and that these are clustered in Wales and the North West of England in particular, and broadly to the west of the Tees-Exe line which by tradition has been used to distinguish the highland from the lowland zones.[74] However, it does not show that there are districts with consistently well below average rates, rather these districts are scattered and their location varies from decade to decade. It is not a simple matter to account for these variations and especially the position of the Welsh districts. What can be

---

[72] Irvine Loudon, *Death in Childbirth: An International Study of Maternal Care and Maternal Mortality, 1800-1950* (Oxford: Clarendon Press, 1992)

[73] Loudon, *Death in Childbirth*, p. 251.

[74] It would be interesting to know whether this broad regional pattern was also apparent in the seventeenth and eighteenth centuries. If it was, then there may be implications for the aggregate findings of parish register based studies which tend to be clustered in the lowland zone. See R. S. Schofield, 'Did the mothers really die? Three centuries of maternal mortality in 'The World We Have Lost'', in L. Bonfield, R. M. Smith and K. Wrightson (eds.), *The World We have Gained: Histories of Population and Social Structure* (Oxford: Blackwell, 1986), pp. 231-260. All but one of the 13 parishes used by Schofield fall to the south and east of the Tees-Exe line, but see also Chris Wilson and Robert Woods, 'Fertility in England: a long-term perspective', *Population Studies* 45 (1991), pp. 399-415, especially pp. 408-409 which gives the location of 25 parishes for which there are family reconstitution studies (7 of the 25 are clearly in the highland zone).

Map 24a. Maternal mortality rate, England and Wales

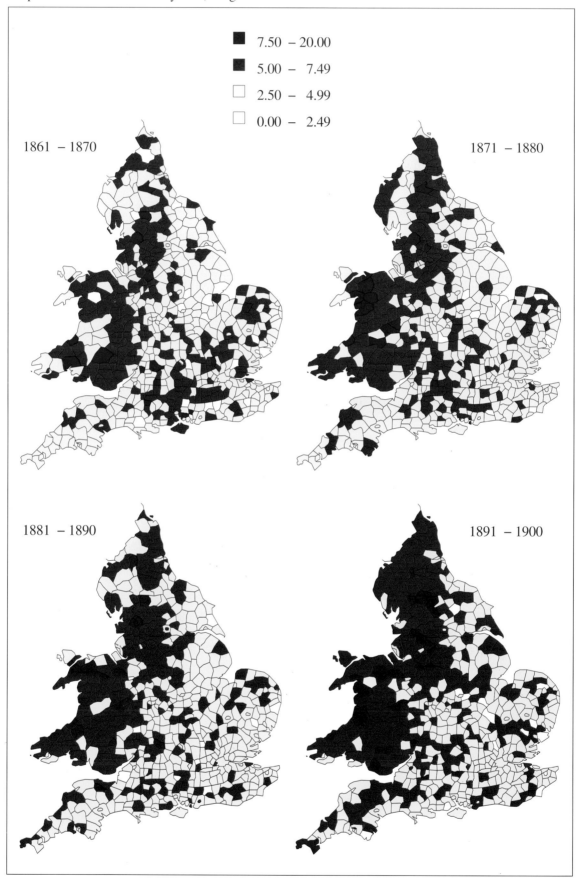

Map 24b. Maternal mortality rate, London

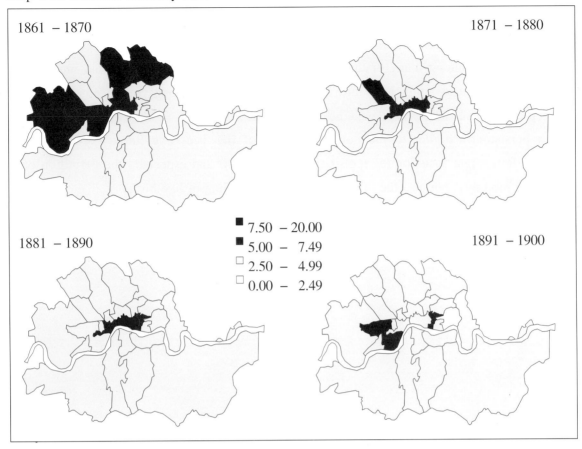

1861 – 1870

1871 – 1880

■ 7.50 – 20.00
■ 5.00 – 7.49
□ 2.50 – 4.99
□ 0.00 – 2.49

1881 – 1890

1891 – 1900

said is that maternal mortality rates were not consistently higher in urban industrial centres; that they did not vary negatively and significantly with the relative distribution of members of the medical profession; but it is possible to speculate, using the evidence of Figure 36, that among many of the Welsh districts persistently high maternal mortality coincided with persistently high rates of Phthisis mortality among young females. It is also probably not merely a coincidence that in general marital fertility appears to have been persistently higher to the north and west of the Tees-Exe line.[75] Alternative explanations might focus on the registration system itself and especially the definition of maternal mortality, but also the full and consistent recording of live births.

[75] Woods, 'Approaches to the fertility transition', Figure 6, p. 300.

10

Death in old age

When did old age begin in Victorian England? Clearly this is not a simple question and perhaps not even a reasonable one. Table 3 indicates that not only could a new born baby in Victorian England expect to live 40 years on average, but also that were such a child to reach its twentieth birthday then it might expect to live a further 40 years, and on reaching its sixtieth birthday a further 12 to 13 years could be anticipated. Whereas today we might think of anyone aged eighty or over as 'old', in the late nineteenth century the age of sixty would have been closer to the mark. It is also worth re-emphasising that of those babies born alive in the 1850s only 40 per cent reached their sixtieth and less that 10 per cent their eightieth birthdays. Also that the mortality rate in old age hardly changed at all between the 1850s and the 1890s. This is clear from Table 3, Figure 2 and also Figure 39 where it is described in greater detail. The stability of the mortality curve for older ages is as important as the lack of radical change in the infant mortality rate before 1900 for the only moderately slow rise of life expectancy in the nineteenth century.

We shall focus here on the two age groups 55-64 and 65-74 since these capture most that may reasonably be said about mortality in old age.

As would be expected the chances of living those extra few years in old age were consistently lower in the large cities than the countryside (Figure 40 and Maps 25a and 25b). In the case of Birmingham Borough there is an interesting relationship between the seasonality of deaths to those aged sixty and over and those deaths attributed to respiratory disease (Figure 32).

In terms of cause of death, it is clear from Figure 6 that death in very old age was dominated by the Other causes category in which many deaths were merely reported as due to old age itself without further elaboration (see Map 6). But for the two age groups with which we are going to deal in this chapter rather more detail is available for the districts. Cancer together with Diseases of the Nervous (Brain), Circulatory (Heart) and Respiratory (Lung) systems are the most prominent causes of death reported. Their full age profiles are shown in Figure 41. Of the four Cancer is perhaps the most interesting, but least significant demographically. Cancer and heart disease are essentially diseases of adulthood and old age while those of the Respiratory and Nervous systems are also prominent in childhood (see Maps 9, 10, 18 and 19). In the cases of the Circulatory and Nervous systems there is very little change in terms of the age-mortality profile from the

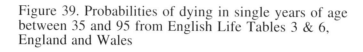

Figure 39. Probabilities of dying in single years of age
between 35 and 95 from English Life Tables 3 & 6,
England and Wales

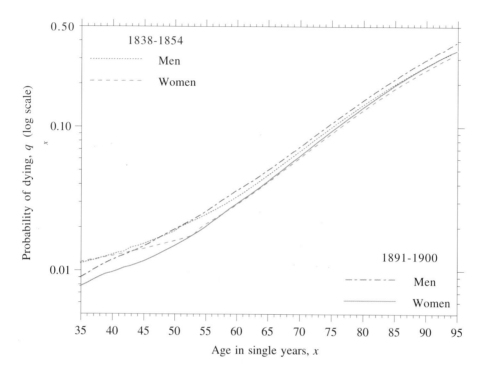

1850s to the 1890s (except that young adult mortality did decline in the latter) or
differences between males and females; stability which is clearly generalised for all causes
of death in Figure 39.

Neither Cancer nor Diseases of the Heart are particularly sensitive to differences in the
urban-rural environment, in fact heart disease is at its highest in certain rural districts
(Figure 42 and Map 26). But this is not the case with Diseases of the Brain and certainly
not with Diseases of the Lung (Figure 43 and Map 27) for which the urban effect is
particularly noticeable. (Figure 32 for Birmingham helps to illustrate just why this should
be so.)[76]

As we have already indicated, three of these causes of death display remarkable
stability and little gender variation, but Cancer mortality does appear to have increased
during the half-century and there were differences between males and females in terms of

[76] Diseases of the Brain appear remarkably low in Wales where the percentage of deaths in old age due to
Other causes was especially high (see Chapter 4 and Map 6).

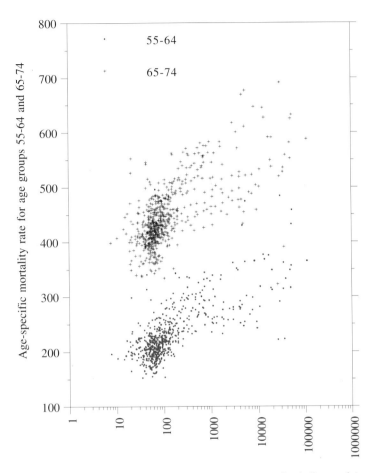

Figure 40. Relationship between mortality rates
for age groups 55-64 and 65-74, and population
density, England and Wales, 1861-1870

Population density, 1861   (persons per sq. km.) (log scale)

rates.[77] For the age group 55-64, Map 28 shows the ratio of male to female Cancer
mortality in the 1860s (comparable with Map 23 for the sex ratio of Phthisis mortality in
early adulthood). Certainly there are some districts with excess male Cancer mortality, but
regional clusters are not obvious outside mid-Wales, the northern Pennines and parts of
the East Midlands.

In general and apart from Diseases of the Lung, variations in mortality beyond age 55
are rather difficult to interpret. Perhaps it is unwise, therefore, to attach too much
significance to those differentials that do appear.

[77] There was considerable debate during the 1890s about the apparent rise in cancer mortality. See George
King and Arthur Newsholme, 'On the alleged increase of cancer', *Journal of the Institute of Actuaries* 36
(1893), pp. 120-150 (also *Proceedings of the Royal Society of London* 54 (1893)), and Newsholme,
'Statistics of cancer'. King and Newsholme (p. 137) conclude that: '1. Males and females suffer equally
from cancer in those parts of the body common to man and woman, the greater prevalence of cancer among
females being due entirely to cancer of the sexual organs, viz., the mamma, ovaries, uterus, and vagina. 2.
The apparent increase in cancer is confined to what we have called "inaccessible" cancer. 3. The increase in
cancer is only apparent and not real, and is due to improvement in diagnosis and more careful certification
of the causes of death. This is shown by the fact that the whole of the increase has taken place in
inaccessible cancer difficult of diagnosis, while accessible cancer easily diagnosed has remained practically
stationary.'

Map 25a. Mortality rate ages 65 – 74, England and Wales

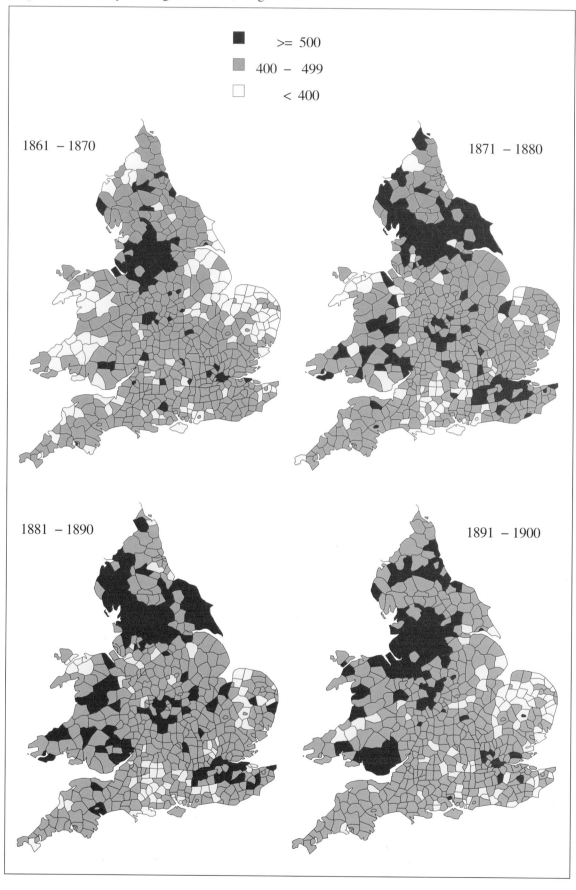

Map 25b. Mortality rate ages 65 – 74, London

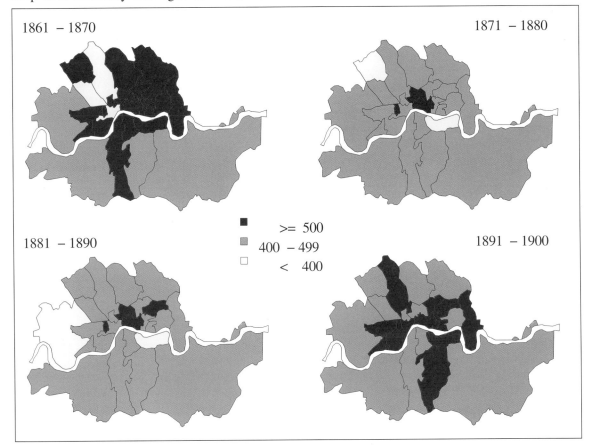

1861 – 1870

1871 – 1880

■ >= 500

400 – 499

□ < 400

1881 – 1890

1891 – 1900

Figure 41. Age-specific mortality rates from Cancer and Diseases of the Circulatory (Heart), Nervous (Brain) and Respiratory (Lung) systems, males and females compared, England and Wales, 1851-1860 and 1891-1900

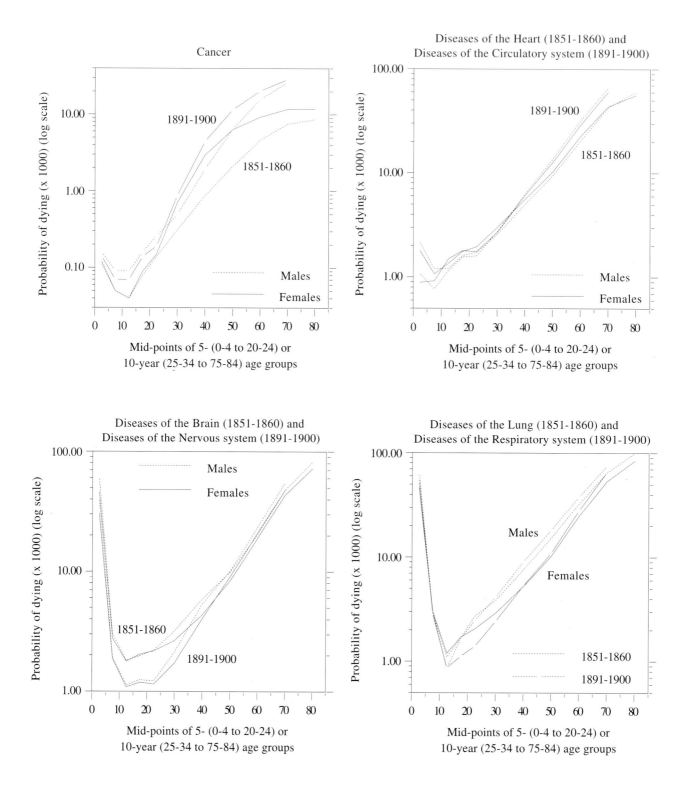

124

Figure 42. Relationships between Cancer and Diseases of the Heart
mortality rates for age group 65-74 and population density,
England and Wales, 1861-1870

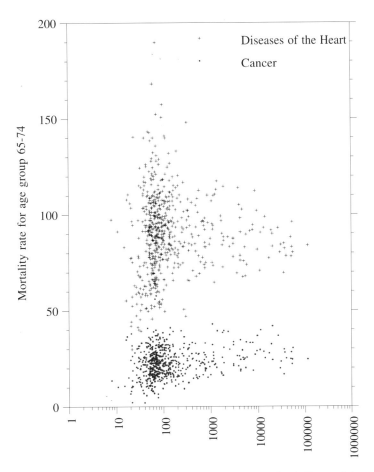

Population density, 1861 (persons per sq. km.) (log scale)

Map 26. Cancer and Diseases of the Heart mortality rate ages 65 – 74, 1861 – 1870

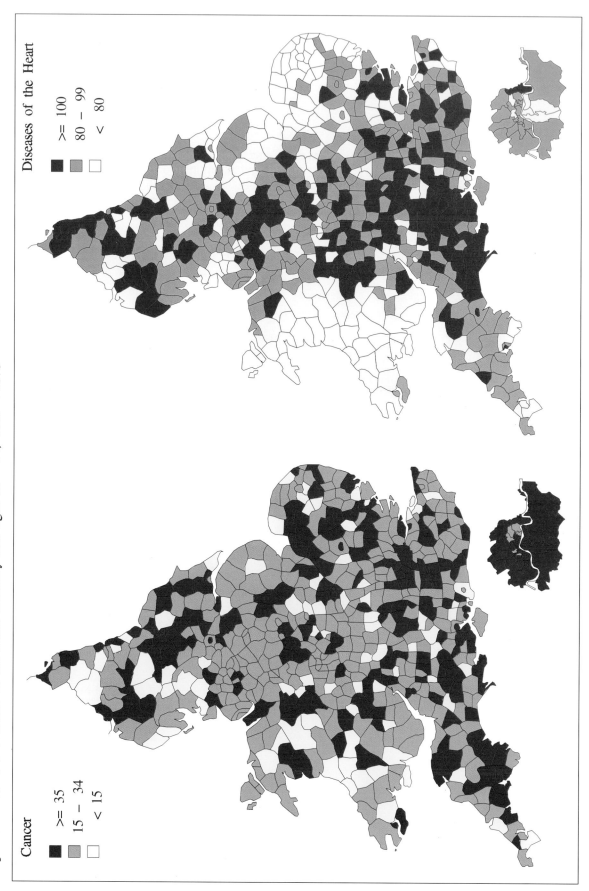

Cancer

■ >= 35
▨ 15 – 34
□ < 15

Diseases of the Heart

■ >= 100
▨ 80 – 99
□ < 80

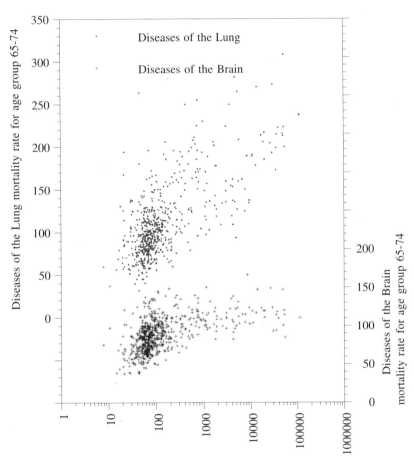

Figure 43. Relationships between Diseases of the
Brain and Lung mortality rates for age group 65-74
and population density, England and Wales, 1861-1870

Map 27. Diseases of the Brain and Diseases of the Lung mortality rate ages 65 – 74, 1861 – 1870

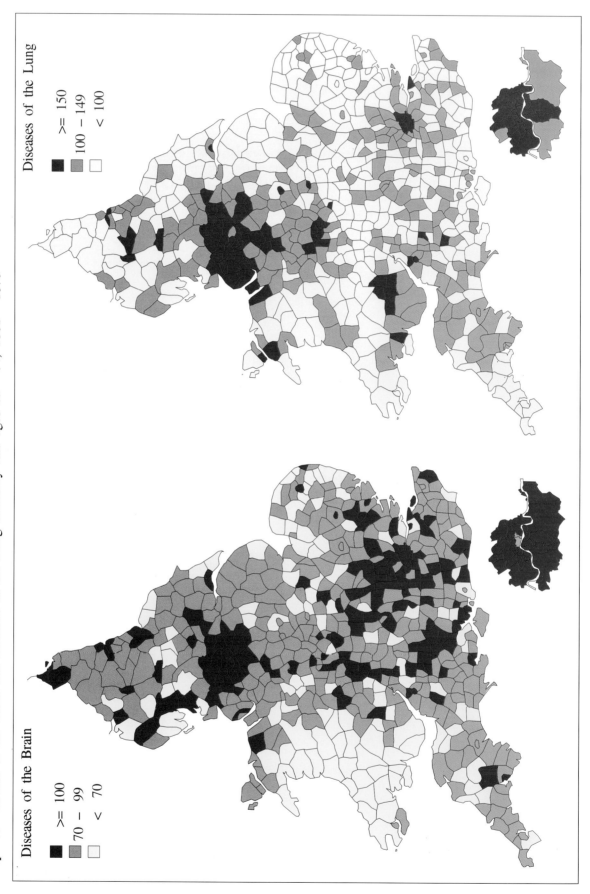

Diseases of the Brain

■ >= 100
▨ 70 – 99
□ < 70

Diseases of the Lung

■ >= 150
▨ 100 – 149
□ < 100

Map 28. Ratio of male to female Cancer mortality rate ages 55 – 64, 1861 – 1870

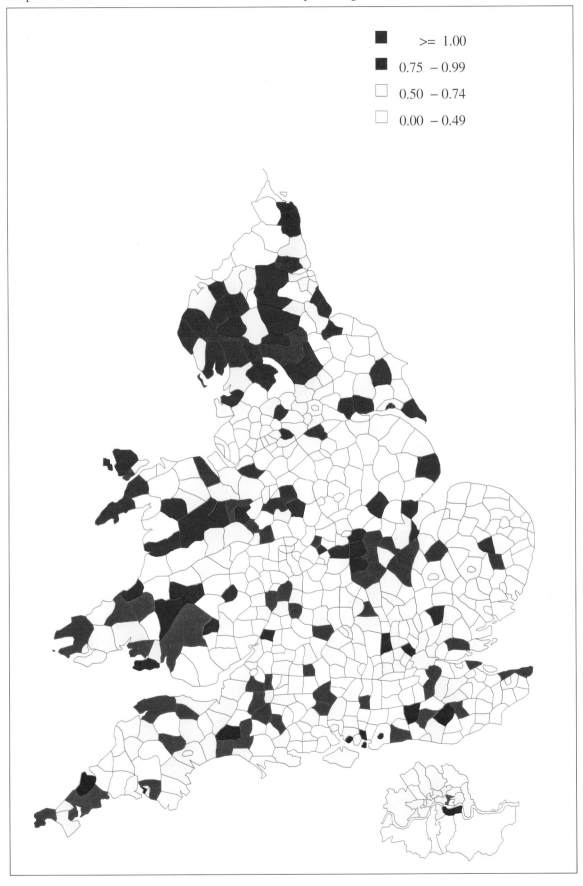

11

Violence and suicide

The *Decennial Supplements* distinguish Violent deaths in the 1850s, Suicide and Other violent deaths in the 1860s and 1870s, and Violence from the 1880s. Here we shall focus mainly on Suicide in the 1860s when it is possible to compare the experiences of females and males.

There has already been a considerable amount of interest shown in Victorian suicide from the statistical and sociological points of view. The former was inspired by the work of Dr William Ogle, Statistical Superintendent at the General Register Office London, and the latter by Emile Durkheim's classic account.[78] It is clear from these studies that the suicide rate varied substantially by age, sex and occupation;[79] and it may be supposed that violent deaths in general, especially accidents and homicides, also displayed strong regularities in these three dimensions. Figure 44 captures some of these variations. It shows the Suicide and Other violent deaths rates by age for males and females in the 1860s. Clearly suicide is of only minor importance demographically, although there certainly are age and sex patterns, but only Other violent deaths among males can be said to be important as a cause of death.

What of the geography of suicide? Olive Anderson summarises her analysis as follows, 'In short, there is indeed a geography of suicide in Victorian and Edwardian England and Wales, although not a deeply defined one; but it is a geography which must be understood in terms of local traditions as well as occupational settings, and which certainly should not be equated with any simple contrasts between·urban and industrial as opposed to rural and agricultural ways of life'.[80] Like John Netten Radcliffe in the 1850s, Anderson uses countics to illustrate her point. Maps 29 and 30 use districts for the 1860s and focus on the age group 55-64.

Map 29 adds a little detail to those county maps prepared by Radcliffe for 1856-1858 and Anderson for 1901-1910. Like them it shows higher rates of suicide in Sussex and Kent, parts of the East Midlands but especially Leicestershire and Northamptonshire, and

[78] William Ogle, 'Suicides in England and Wales in relation to age, sex, season and occupation', *Journal of the Statistical Society* 49 (1886), pp. 101-135, Emile Durkheim, *Le Suicide. Etude de Sociologie* (Paris: Félix Alcan, 1897), and more recently, Olive Anderson, *Suicide in Victorian and Edwardian England* (Oxford: Clarendon Press, 1987).

[79] The occupational dimension cannot be considered here, but see Anderson, *Suicide*, and Woods, 'Physician, heal thyself'.

[80] Anderson, *Suicide*, p. 103. Here Anderson follows John Netten Radcliffe, 'On the distribution of suicides in England and Wales', *Journal of Psychological Medicine* 11 (1859), pp. 582-602, although she does use registration district data for the 1860s to draw out the relative lack of distinction between suicide rates in urban and rural places (pp. 87-93).

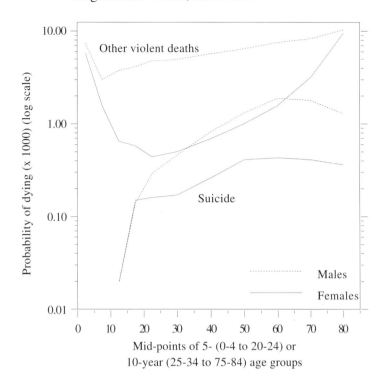

Figure 44. Age-specific mortality rates from Suicide
and Other violent deaths males and females compared,
England and Wales, 1861-1870

what is now Cumbria. However as Anderson found, suicide rates are especially difficult to interpret in ecological terms; while certain forms of occupation may be geographically concentrated as may some means (especially drowning) detailed analysis of motivation is not necessarily enhanced by considering local variations.[81]

Other violent deaths, on the other hand, do show clearer signs of concentration in districts that are likely to have had employment structures where accidents were common especially among males. Map 30 shows that the Other violent deaths rate for ages 55-64 in the 1860s was at its highest in the north and west of England and Wales, but particularly some of those areas associated with mining or quarrying. In other cases rates could appear higher as a result of chance occurrences such as road or rail accidents or drownings, and do not necessarily reflect the extent of exposure to higher average risks.

[81] There is an intriguing, but perhaps deceptive coincidence in the East Midlands between excess male Cancer mortality (Map 28) and suicide mortality (Map 29).

131

Map 29. Suicide mortality rate ages 55 – 64, 1861 – 1870

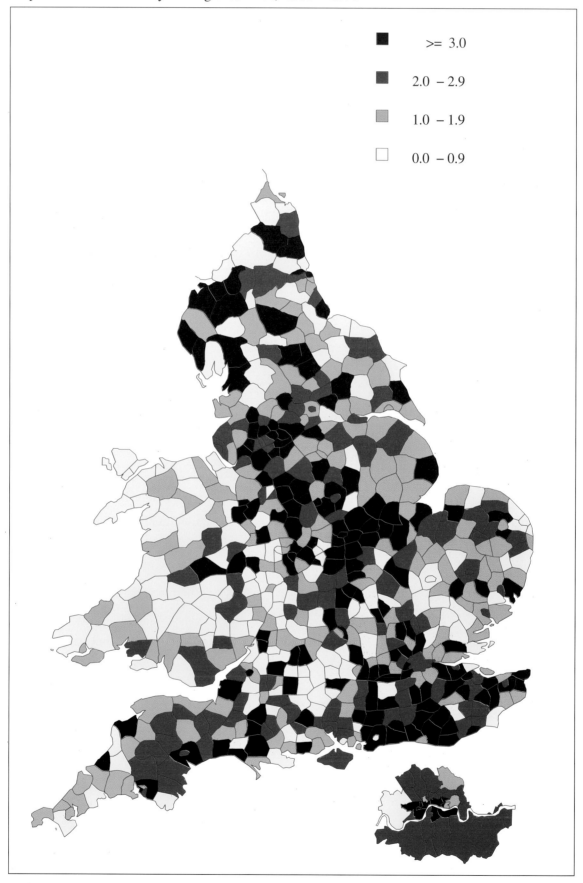

■ >= 3.0

■ 2.0 – 2.9

■ 1.0 – 1.9

□ 0.0 – 0.9

Map 30. Other violent deaths mortality rate ages 55 – 64, 1861 – 1870

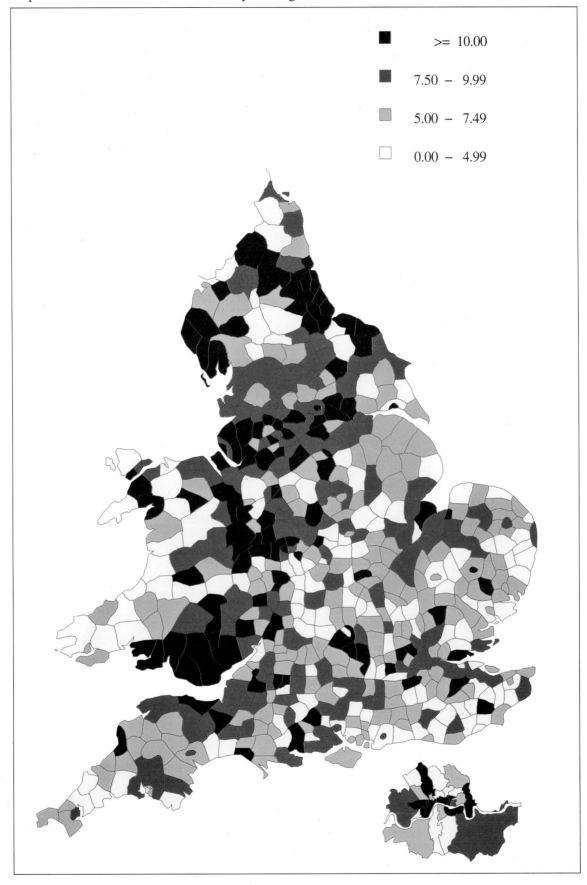

12

Gender

Differences in the experiences of males and females have often been highlighted in historical studies although today the life chances of males are inferior to those of females at every age, this has not always been the case.[82] This chapter while drawing together some of the points already made about the influence of gender on mortality patterns (summarised in Figures 6, 7 and 30) focuses especially on the different mortality experiences of males and females of the same ages living in the same districts.

First, let us establish at which ages and when was there excess mortality among males and females. Figure 45 uses the q_x function (the probability of dying at exact age x) from the full English Life Tables for 1838-1854 and 1891-1900 (ELTs 3 and 6, see Tables 3 and 4) and those developed for the so-called healthy registration districts of England and Wales. Females experienced excess mortality between the ages of 10 and 40 at mid-century, but only 10 and 15 by its last decade. However, in the Healthy Districts where mortality was substantially lower (by approximately 8 years in terms of life expectancy at birth), females spent a longer period of their lives liable to experience higher mortality rates that males.[83] Clearly it is in the teenage years where one might expect to encounter persistent female excess mortality, but does this excess display a distinctive geographical pattern?

Map 31 shows the ratio of male to female total mortality rates for the age groups 10-14 and 15-19 in the 1860s. In relation to deaths under age 15, which would not have been affected by the perils of maternal mortality, Michael Anderson has argued that, 'Much of the excess [female] mortality, particularly in rural areas, was due to high levels of respiratory tuberculosis, and the pattern on a registration district and county basis reveals that poor agricultural areas, and districts with large unskilled working-class populations, were especially affected. This in turn suggests that part of the responsibility

---

[82] See Michael Anderson, 'The social implications of demographic change', in F. M. L. Thompson (ed.) *The Cambridge Social History of Britain, 1750-1950, Volume 2, People and their Environment* (Cambridge: Cambridge University Press, 1990), pp. 1-70, especially pp. 18-19, and Jane Humphries, ''Bread and a pennyworth of treacle': excess female mortality in England in the 1840s', *Cambridge Journal of Economics* 15 (1991), pp. 451-473. Jacques Vallin, 'Mortality in Europe from 1720 to 11914: long-term trends and changes in patterns by age and sex', in Roger Schofield, David Reher and Alain Bideau (eds.), *The Decline of Mortality in Europe* (Oxford: Clarendon Press, 1991), pp. 38-67, especially p. 65, and Dominique Tabutin, 'La surmortalité féminine en Europe avant 1940', *Population* 33 (1) (1978), pp. 121-148, trace changes in the demography of excess mortality.

[83] Figures 30 and 45 exemplify the following problem: a 20 year old woman living in a low mortality rural district would face a higher risk of dying than her male counter-part, but if she moved to a high mortality town her actual survival chances would be reduced although she would be better placed than men of her age in that town.

Figure 45. The ratio of male to female probabilities of dying
(q_xs for single years), England and Wales and Healthy Districts

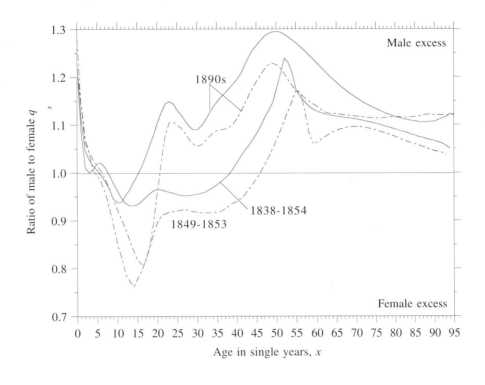

England and Wales, 1838-1854   England and Wales, 1891-1900

Healthy Districts, 1849-1853   Healthy Districts, 1891-1900

lies with low levels of nutrition, particularly during the adolescent growth spurt, a by-product of a contemporary insistence on trying to keep the male 'breadwinner' well fed even during hard times; it is noticeable in this context that other areas with high excess rates were mining districts where the same culturally maintained bias in food allocation seems to have been present.'[84] Girls and women may also have spent a longer period indoors and their role as carers for the sick may also have been relevant in this context.

It is no simple matter to demonstrate the value of these points. Certainly it can be shown in which districts female mortality was in excess of that for males aged 10-19 and this is done in Map 32 by classifying districts according to whether excess female mortality was experienced at both 10-14 and 15-19 in the 1860s. It is also possible to illustrate the extent to which excess female mortality was faced mainly in the countryside and whether differential Phthisis mortality also played a part. Figure 46 begins by relating the ratio of male to female 15-19 mortality to the ratio of male to female Phthisis 20-24 mortality (see Map 23), but it also distinguishes those 206 districts that lost population between 1861 and 1911. It is not surprising that many of those districts whose female

---

[84] Anderson, 'Social implications', p. 19.

Map 31. Ratio of male to female mortality ages 10 – 14 and 15 – 19, 1861 – 1870

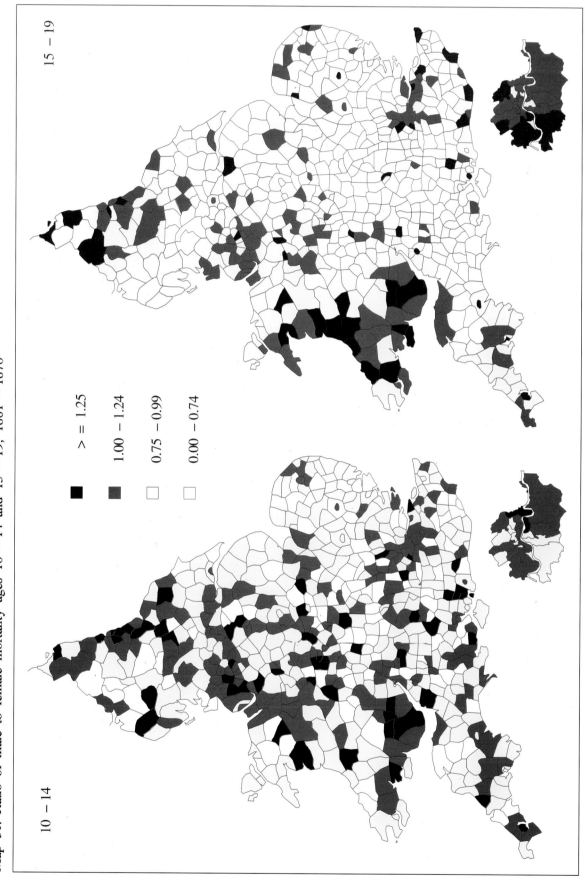

10 – 14

15 – 19

> = 1.25

1.00 – 1.24

0.75 – 0.99

0.00 – 0.74

Map 32. Categories of excess female mortality ages 10 – 19, 1861 – 1870

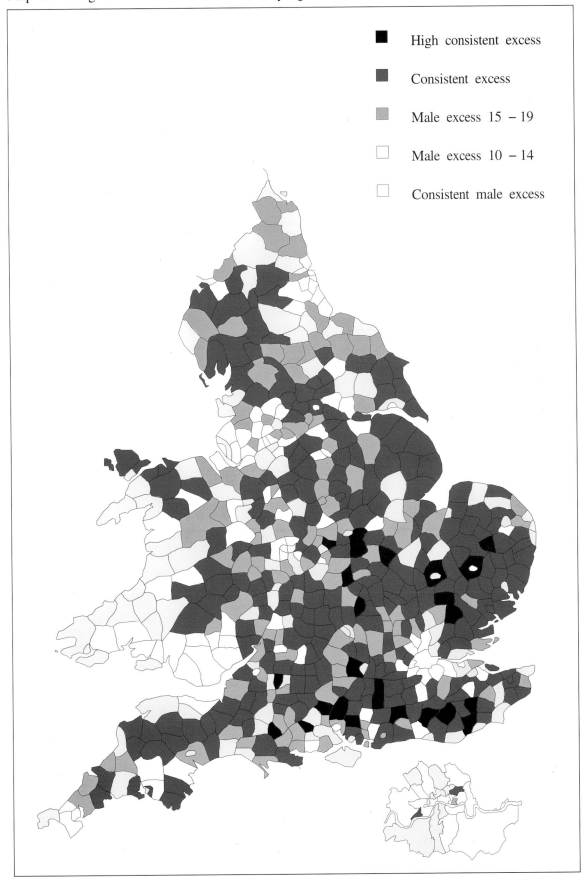

High consistent excess

Consistent excess

Male excess 15 – 19

Male excess 10 – 14

Consistent male excess

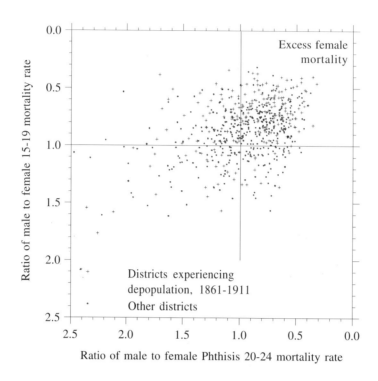

Figure 46. Ratio of male to female 15-19 mortality
rates against ratio of male to female Phthisis 20-24
mortality rates, England and Wales, 1861-1870

populations experienced excess mortality in general also suffered excess Phthisis
mortality in early adulthood, but it may also be significant that a substantial group of
these same districts were both rural and subject to depopulation in the late nineteenth
century. Figure 47 helps to develop the point by showing the relationship between an
index of mortality derived for the 15-19 age group and population density.[85] Clearly
excess female mortality was almost exclusively a rural phenomenon at mid-century, but
not all rural districts experienced such excess. In this respect mortality appears to differ
from literacy, which can be used to provide a parallel perspective on access to education
and which may be indexed in a similar way. Its variation is also illustrated in Figure 47.[86]
While excess female mortality was to be found in the countryside, excess female illiteracy
was mainly an urban phenomenon.

Figures 46 and 47 appear to highlight an anomalous relationship if one wishes to
account for mortality differentials strictly in terms of economic behaviour and human
capital. Why invest in the education of females so that they are more nearly on a par with

[85] The method of indexing uses orthogonal regression techniques and replicates the approach adopted by
Humphries, 'Bread', pp. 458-459, with data for the registration counties of England and Wales.

[86] Literacy, or rather illiteracy, is measured by the percentage of men and women signing the marriage
register with a mark in 1861. This is far from ideal, but it does have the advantage of allowing geographical
and temporal variations to be charted. See R. I. Woods, 'Approaches to the fertility transition in Victorian
England', *Population Studies* 41 (1987), pp. 283-311, especially p. 296. Literacy has been indexed in the
same way as mortality using orthogonal regression.

Figure 47. Indices of literacy and mortality against population density, England and Wales

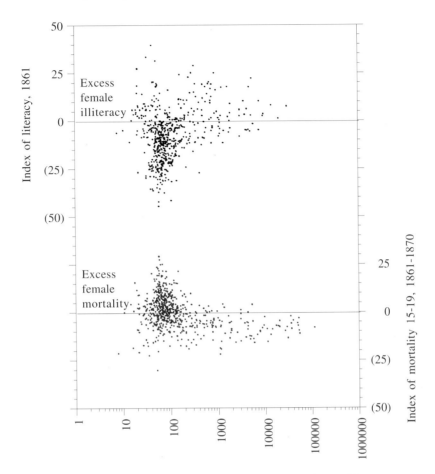

Population density, 1861 (persons per sq. km.) (log scale)

or superior to males when differential disinvestment in their health sets them at a relative disadvantage? It is likely that ecological analysis cannot offer an answer to this question, but merely to pose it may help to set enquiries on an alternative track. Perhaps one approach would be to consider in greater detail the effects of age-, sex- and health-selective migration from those rural districts which experienced migration loss or even absolute depopulation. The employers of female domestic servants might have been far more sensitive to the long-term health of their maids and those young women who were obviously unfit would have had little opportunity but to stay at home despite being reasonably well-educated.

Figure 48 illustrates more clearly the weak but significant negative relationship between the mortality and literacy indices. It also shows differences within the distribution among districts experiencing the following migration trends between 1851 and 1911: (1) depopulation, (2) constant migration loss, (3) fluctuating migration trends, (4) gain followed by loss, (5) loss followed by gain, and (6) constant gain (see Map 34). There

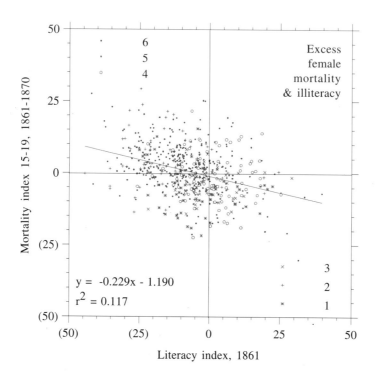

Figure 48. Classification of districts in terms of
mortality and literacy indices, England and Wales

were districts where both mortality and literacy differentials were to women's disadvantage and these are labelled 'worst' in Map 33 (districts in the upper right quadrant of Figure 48), but there were also districts in which relative mortality and literacy levels were to women's advantage and these are described as 'best' in Map 33 (lower left quadrant of Figure 48). Although there is at least one very distinct cluster of 'worst' districts in the North of England, no very clear pattern emerges.

Work on gender differentials in health, mortality and access to education is in an early stage of development. Here we have offered a brief examination of just a few of the complex problems that will need to be considered by focusing on geographical variations for the ages 10-19, and by setting mortality differentials alongside those related to illiteracy. While there is certainly a case for considering such geographical variations in greater detail, it remains to be seen how they relate to differential treatment in the workplace and at home. It also appears evident that mortality differentials between males and females may not be stable from age group to age group, that they may change over time, and that they may differ from other possible dimensions of disadvantage, education for instance, in the nineteenth century.

140

Map 33. Categories of 'worst' and 'best' districts for women from Figure 48, 1861 – 1870

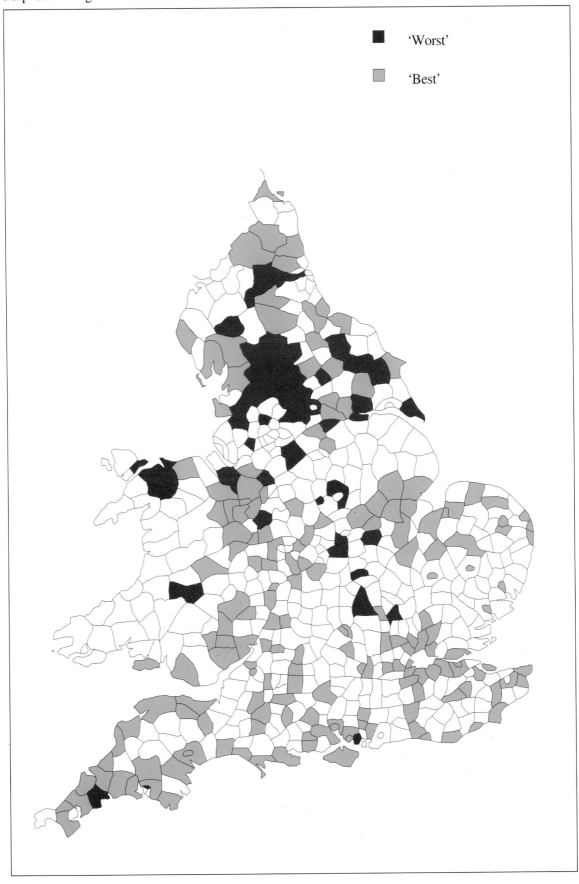

■ 'Worst'

▪ 'Best'

13

Places and diseases

Where one lived in Victorian England critically affected not only one's life chances, but also the manner in which death might occur. This has been clearly demonstrated by the maps and figures presented here.[87] But what bearing does this broad and apparently obvious conclusion have on attempts to offer a detailed description of and to account for the course of the European mortality transition? Is the McKeown interpretation still of value? Is the debate between those who emphasise the importance of improving living standards, especially via nutritional status and housing quality, and those who stress the role of public health interventions any closer to resolution? What may now be said of the long-term consequences of urbanisation for the health of a society where there is a persistent urban-rural mortality gradient?

'It would be only a small exaggeration to say that our understanding of historical mortality patterns, and of their causes and implications, is still in its infancy. Despite its importance, we probably know less of mortality than of fertility; there has been a European Fertility Project, but nothing similar exists for mortality. The complexities inherent in the methodological and substantive issues affecting its study have often daunted researchers and together with data problems, have tended to limit progress in this field.'[88] These observations on the state of our understanding of the European mortality transition are still broadly correct. This atlas may even have served to make some of the complexities more obvious. It has shown that even in a small, relatively homogeneous country like England and Wales not only are there sharp and important differences between localities in terms of the level of mortality, that the age component is especially important, but also that cause of death patterns vary with age and location. The more one descends into the detail, the more difficult it becomes to accept the averaging of means which are conventionally used to chart the broad outlines of demographic change and to

---

[87] Some of the mortality patterns identified in this atlas also appear to have persisted into the late twentieth century, although the rates are of course much lower, see Britton, *Mortality and Geography*. It is also worth noting that in the 1990s 'The excess mortality associated with residence in areas designated as deprived by census based indicators is wholly explained by the concentration in those areas of people with adverse personal or household socioeconomic factors.' Andrew Sloggett and Heather Joshi, 'Higher mortality in deprived areas: community or personal disadvantages?', *British Medical Journal* 309 (1994), pp. 1470-1474, quoted from p. 1470. In the 1890s community disadvantage was more important than personal.

[88] Schofield *et al.* (eds.), *Decline of European Mortality*, p. 2. The results of the European Fertility Project are summarised in Ansley J. Coale and Susan Cotts Watkins (eds.), *The Decline of Fertility in Europe* (Princeton: Princeton University Press, 1986).

which the various interpretations relate. The McKeown interpretation perfectly illustrates this and several other epistemological problems.[89]

On the basis of a detailed comparison of national cause of death data for England and Wales between 1848-1854 and 1901 McKeown drew the following conclusions: perhaps half of the total mortality decline could be attributed to rising living standards working especially through the reduction of respiratory tuberculosis; about one quarter was due to the changes introduced by the sanitary reformers, and a further quarter could be attributed to changes in the character of diseases, but especially scarlet fever. McKeown also argued that with the exception of smallpox vaccination, specific preventive and curative measures would have had no significant impact on the decline of mortality before the twentieth century.[90] Most critics while questioning the quality of Victorian cause of death data and the propriety of making inferential leaps from proximate to ultimate cause, also express admiration for the simplicity of McKeown's approach and his 'strong and declarative style'. In terms of the interpretation itself, and to over-simplify somewhat, the debate now focuses on *A* the impact of public health intervention by the State, both national and local, coupled with advances in sanitation technology and the triumph of germ theory or *B* improvements in living standards—real income, nutrition, housing— which had a significant bearing on health and height, and tuberculosis mortality. In *A* there is an emphasis on exposure to disease while in *B* it is resistance that improves. Those who support *B*, the McKeownites, are optimistic about the benefits of industrialisation and rising living standards in the nineteenth century while at the same time pointing out the failure of infant mortality to decline, while the advocates of *A* are convinced that living standards only began to improve in the last three decades of the century and that there is little convincing direct evidence that the quantity and quality of food intake actually improved sufficiently to have had a major impact on disease resistance.[91]

If this were only a two-horse race, then the material presented here would tend not to favour *B* while at the same time remaining unconvinced by all the claims made for *A*. The description of Phthisis mortality presented in Chapter 8 clearly supports the view that there was indeed a substantial reduction in pulmonary tuberculosis in the second half of the nineteenth century, that this was a real decline and not merely a matter of nosology or statistical accountancy. But it is not consistent with the *B*-type argument that improving nutritional status in particular was responsible for enhanced resistance unless, that is, one is prepared to believe that such improvements were ubiquitous throughout England. It is far

[89] On the philosophical problems raised by McKeown's approach see especially S. Ryan Johansson, 'Rhetoric and reality in modern mortality history', *Historical Methods* 27 (1994), pp. 101-125.

[90] See Woods, *Population of Britain in the Nineteenth Century*, pp. 44-46.

[91] See Simon Szreter, 'The importance of social intervention in Britain's mortality decline *c.* 1850-1914: a re-interpretation of the role of public health', *Social History of Medicine* 1 (1988), pp. 1-37, Sumit Guha, 'The importance of social intervention in England's mortality decline: the evidence reviewed', *Social History of Medicine* 7 (1994), pp. 89-113, and Simon Szreter, 'Mortality in England in the eighteenth and nineteenth centuries: a reply to Sumit Guha', *Social History of Medicine* 7 (1994), pp. 269-282.

more likely that pulmonary tuberculosis itself became less virulent, that the case fatality rate did indeed decline although exposure to the disease was little affected; that the risk of infection with *tubercle bacilli* did not alter although the risk of development of tuberculosis became less.

There is a long tradition of using mortality statistics to monitor effectiveness and general impact of public health reforms which runs from Farr via Newsholme to the Black Report of 1980. All such endeavours find it difficult to know which index to use for it is on this decision and how the measurement is carried out that the whole debate on quality of health and the presence of inequalities hinges. If one were to select the Diarrhoea & Dysentery infant mortality rate as the principal index of sanitary efficiency then the towns of Victorian England would not be able to demonstrate substantial improvement.[92] Map 8a gives little reason to think that, at least for infants, there had been a sanitary revolution in the nineteenth century. But Map 8a, especially when compared with Map 12a, also epitomises exactly why, for the longer term, *A*-type arguments are more persuasive. Between the 1840s and 1901 the health intervention movement was successful in largely removing some of the worst excesses—cholera and smallpox, for example—and of laying the foundation for rapid improvements in the twentieth century. Without such engineering and administrative infrastructures the infant mortality rate would not have declined so dramatically in the cities in the early years of the twentieth century. But there is little reason to believe that preventive measures directed at the infectious diseases of childhood—measles, whooping cough, scarlet fever and diphtheria—were at all successful in changing their behaviour in the nineteenth and even the first decades of the twentieth century.[93] It also seems likely that air pollution, especially in the cities, remained particularly important as a contributor to respiratory diseases in childhood and old age (Maps 9, 18 and 27). While the domestic consumption of water could be tackled in the nineteenth century, air quality could not be improved while coal was the only source of fuel both domestic and industrial. In general, the impact of health intervention in the Victorian era was somewhat limited although it would certainly be possible to argue that without it matters would have been even worse.

It must also be said that in many respects *A* and *B* offer falsely simple alternatives. First, although in *B* rising living standards may not have operated via tuberculosis to give the outcome proposed, it is nonetheless obvious that average real incomes have increased in the long term and that this has facilitated greater social and personal investment in

---

[92] Local medical officers of health like Newsholme in Brighton were especially frustrated by the increase in diarrhoeal mortality in the 1890s. See Arthur Newsholme, 'A contribution to the study of epidemic diarrhoea', *Public Health* 12 (3) (1899), pp. 139-213, Robert Woods, 'Public health and public hygiene: the urban environment in the late nineteenth and early twentieth centuries', in Roger Schofield *et al.* (eds.) *The Decline of Mortality in Europe* (Oxford: Clarendon Press, 1991), pp. 233-247, and Mooney, 'Did London pass the 'sanitary test'?'

[93] This is the conclusion of Hardy, *Epidemic Streets*, p. 290. None of the evidence presented in Chapter 6 serves to challenge it.

health care without which life expectancy at birth would not have reached 80-plus years in the late twentieth century. Secondly, it should be remembered that the decline of mortality in the nineteenth century was rather modest and that its role as prime mover in the modern rise of population has been exaggerated not only by McKeown, but also and perhaps inadvertently by the critics of his account of the causes of mortality decline.[94] Thirdly, using the pattern of social-class differences in childhood mortality in the United States in the 1890s, Preston and Haines have argued that 'lack of know-how rather than lack of resources was principally responsible for foreshortening life'.[95] The point could also be applied to Victorian England and Wales where local disease environments were even more important than class differentials. Fourthly, in terms of differences in life expectancy at birth the variation among districts (lowest to highest) in 1851 was at least four times greater than the difference between the national life expectancy at birth for that year and its equivalent in 1901, but in the following half-century the increase in life expectancy was roughly equal to what the range had been in 1901.[96] Compared with the geographical variation in mortality, temporal change in the nineteenth century was small indeed.

Let us turn away, therefore, from McKeown's preoccupation with change and reconsider the factors that influenced variation, and especially the consequences of urbanisation. Map 34 summarises the effects of population re-distribution in England and Wales between 1851 and 1911, but especially the role of migration in focusing growth in the South East and the towns of the Midlands, the North of England and South Wales.[97] Outside these districts most of the more remote rural areas and even some of the inner-city districts experienced constant migration loss and in many there was depopulation. Generally speaking, it is these rural districts that are the healthy ones where mortality is at its lowest compared with the urban areas, but not all the groups or causes of death considered in this atlas show clear urban-rural differentials. What exactly was it about the urban districts that made them so much more dangerous than the Victorian countryside?

[94] It seems likely that in sketching his picture of the demographic transition in England and Wales using crude birth (CBR) and death rates (CDR) for 1700-1960, McKeown was influenced by existing diagrams that rely upon John Brownlee's estimates of 1916. These estimates show CBR to be constant before 1870 while CDR declines between 1770 and 1800 and thus only mortality decline is responsible for initiating the modern rise of population. Thomas McKeown and C. R. Lowe, *An Introduction to Social Medicine* (Oxford: Blackwell, 1966), Figure 2, p. 6, The third edition of this text, published in 1984, also shows this graph. See also Wrigley and Schofield, *Population History*, p. 148.

[95] Samuel H. Preston and Michael R. Haines, *Fatal Years: Child Mortality in Late Nineteenth-Century America* (Princeton: Princeton University Press, 1991), p. 209.

[96] Raymond Illsley and Julian Le Grand, 'Regional inequalities in mortality', *Journal of Epidemiology and Community Health* 47 (1993), pp. 444-449 provide an interesting contribution to the health inequalities debate by considering trends in regional differentials in age-specific mortality measures post-1931. In the nineteenth century such differentials would have been higher in general, and especially so for the young and old.

[97] Map 34 is based on Lawton, 'Population changes in England and Wales', Figure 6, p. 64.

Map 34. Migration trends, 1851 – 1911

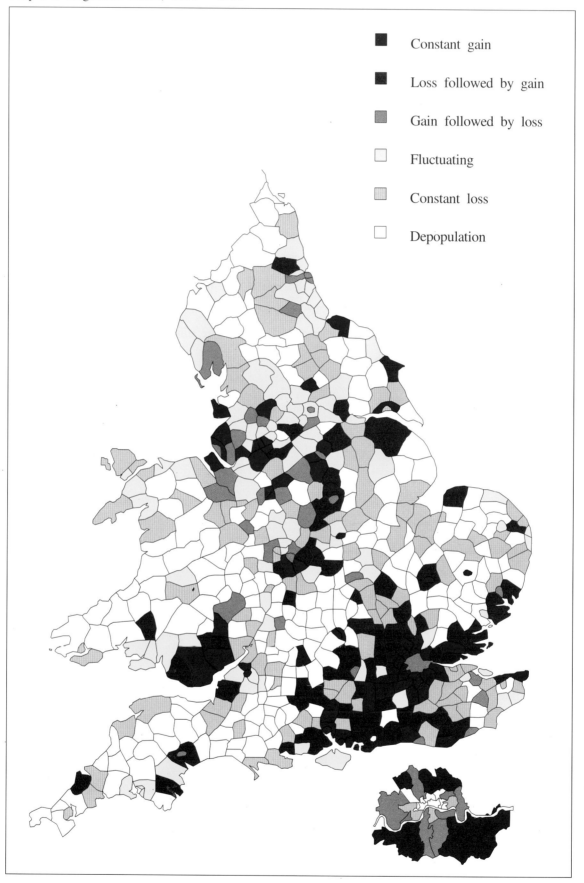

Constant gain

Loss followed by gain

Gain followed by loss

Fluctuating

Constant loss

Depopulation

Figure 49. Relationship between life expectancy at birth in years and population size of English and Welsh districts, 1861

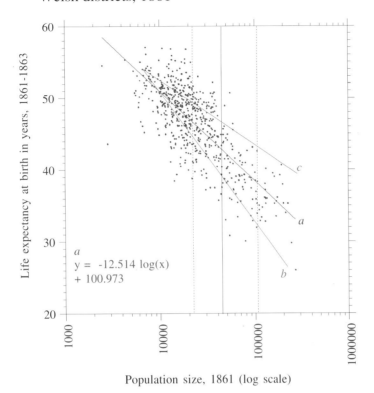

Population size, 1861 (log scale)

In infancy Diarrhoea & Dysentery (Figure 16) and Diseases of the Lung (Respiratory system), and in old age Diseases of the Lung (Figure 43) were especially important in establishing and maintaining the urban-rural mortality differential. However, it is the infectious diseases of early childhood that are most sensitive to differences in population density and environment. Measles (Figure 25) and Scarlet fever (Figure 26), for example, show most clearly why there was such a pronounced mortality gradient in the nineteenth century between town and country. For the early 1860s we are able to illustrate in Figure 49 the general form of that gradient in terms of life expectancy at birth.[98] Figure 49 also shows the effects of population concentration in the cities. Each of the three vertical lines distinguishes a quarter of the population of England and Wales in 1861. The concentration of more and more people in those districts to the right of the central line during the nineteenth century symbolises the effects of urbanisation on the national average level of mortality working through the mortality gradient.[99] Since national levels

[98] Figure 49 is reminiscent of 'Farr's law', although Farr used crude death rates and population density. See the following: *Supplement* to the *Twenty-fifth Annual Report*; Farr, *Vital Statistics*, pp. 172-176; and John Brownlee, 'Density and death-rate: Farr's law', *Journal of the Royal Statistical Society* 83 (1920), pp. 280-283.

[99] Robert Woods, 'The effects of population redistribution on the level of mortality in nineteenth-century England and Wales', *Journal of Economic History* 45 (1985), pp. 645-651, explores this problem at greater length.

of life expectancy at birth did improve in the second half of the nineteenth century while population growth and urbanisation also continued, the slope of the regression line in Figure 49 must also have become less steep as mortality in the cities was reduced (a to c). However, it may also be the case that urban mortality was especially high in the 1840s, 1850s and 1860s as the result of a cyclical increase in the virulence of some of the infectious diseases of childhood, especially scarlet fever, and that urban growth made others, like measles and whooping cough, far more prominent in the tally of causes of death than they had formerly been (represented by b).

It is interesting to speculate about the longer-term effects of population re-distribution in an environment where there is a persistent urban-rural mortality gradient. One possibility is shown in Figure 50. It uses the sort of material illustrated in Figure 3 in the form of a conventional two-dimensional graph (percentage of the population of England and Wales (z dimension) living in districts with given levels of life expectancy at birth (x dimension)), but adds the further axis of time (y dimension) to create a three-dimensional image.[100] In the sixteenth and seventeenth centuries when urbanisation was at a relatively low level, the higher mortality found in the towns, especially London, had only a minor influence on the national average, but in the eighteenth and nineteenth centuries the continued growth of London together with the dramatic expansion of the provincial commercial and industrial centres probably retarded the decline of national mortality. In the twentieth century mortality declined rapidly and most people now live in districts with high life expectancy at birth. Figure 50 helps to illustrate not only the prevailing level of mortality, but also the effect of variation among geographical units. Before the mid-eighteenth century the ridge is narrow, sharp and straight; then it broadens out and gradually begins to swing; and finally the ridge narrows and sharpens again as the swing towards very low levels of mortality is accentuated.

Figure 50 offers one very simple way of envisioning the outcome of a highly complex process in which the effects of industrialisation, population growth and re-distribution acted in an interactive and cumulative fashion via urban growth and urbanisation. We know in charting this process that it is important to distinguish between age groups—especially infants and children, young adults and the old—and between secular and cyclical effects, but this atlas has also helped to suggest ways in which the impact of urbanisation would have manifest itself in distinctive age- and cause-specific ways. For example, while nearly all areas experienced the decline, which may have been continuous throughout the nineteenth century, in pulmonary tuberculosis mortality among those in early adulthood, the towns and especially the

---

[100] Figure 50 is entirely speculative before 1851 where it relies on the estimates of life expectancy at birth provided by Wrigley and Schofield, *Population History of England.*, and guesswork for the distribution of population, although see E. A. Wrigley, *People, Cities and Wealth* (Oxford: Blackwell, 1987), p. 170.

Figure 50. Three-dimensional display of the effects of population redistribution on life expectancy at birth in years, England and Wales, 1551-2001

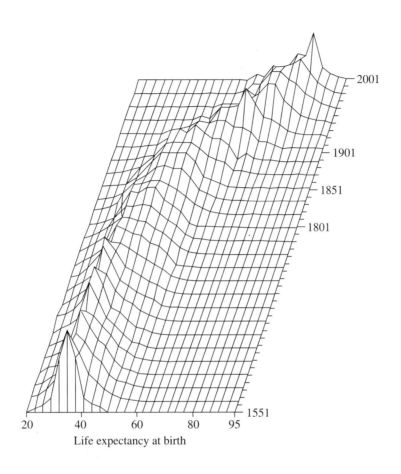

Life expectancy at birth

largest urban centres probably experienced increased mortality in early childhood from the common infectious diseases during the middle decades of the nineteenth century. Mortality which was over and above both that due to the water-borne diseases which proved so lethal to infants and the old, and which were the principal target for the sanitarians, and the respiratory diseases in general which especially afflicted the urban poor and the old in winter.[101]

[101] Jeffrey G. Williamson, *Coping with City Growth during the British Industrial Revolution* (Cambridge: Cambridge University Press, 1990) presents a number of elegant arguments concerning the trade-off between higher wage rates and employment opportunities set against higher urban mortality. It now seems clear that it was the rural-urban migrants' young or shortly to be born children who were most disadvantaged in terms of life chances. It is also the case that young female migrants who were generally at a mortality disadvantage compared with men in the countryside would put themselves at a relative advantage by moving to town while increasing their actual risk of dying young compared with their rural sisters (see Chapter 12).

149

Figure 51. Three-dimensional displays of the total number
of deaths, deaths from respiratory disease and deaths from
diarrhoea per week, Birmingham Borough, 1880-1901

All deaths

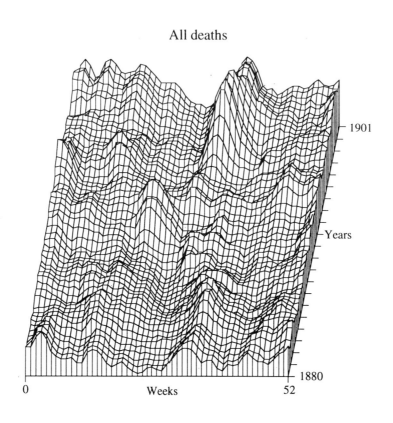

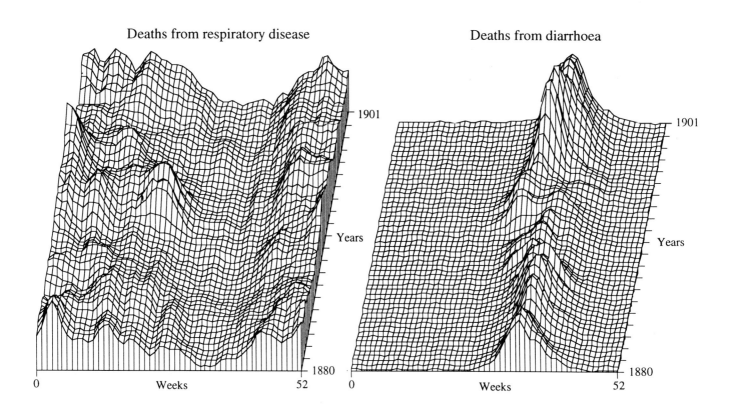

While Figure 50 provides an interesting way of illustrating the changing interplay between mortality and the distribution of population in different disease environments, the particular experience of individual towns is also worth emphasising. In this atlas we have used London to show how cause-specific mortality patterns have varied at the intra-urban level and Birmingham Borough to illustrate the seasonal incidence of disease. Figure 51 uses the example of Birmingham again to show the highly distinctive nature of the urban disease environment.[102] In this case the 52 weeks of the year provide the x dimension, the y dimension is given by the 22 years from 1880 to 1901 and the z dimension is the number of deaths. The three-dimensional surfaces created are rugged and inhospitable: neither the winter nor the summer is safe and although there is some distinct seasonality, there may also be some trend from year to year in the severity of the seasons. Figure 51 uses three examples: all deaths, deaths due to respiratory diseases and those from diarrhoea. But for deaths due to diarrhoea the weeks of summer would experience very low mortality, although as we have already shown (see Figures 17 and 18) it is diarrhoeal mortality particularly in infancy that makes the cities so lethal especially in the 1890s. Every summer there is a ridge of additional risk to be crossed for young children and every year winter and spring are also hazardous for the old. It is through these seasonal extremes that the urban disease environment exacts its characteristically heavy toll.[103]

[102] Figures 50 and 51 were drawn using MacGridzo which is designed to create a 3-dimensional surface using observations for points with east-west and north-south co-ordinates. The surface smoothing procedure in the software may create some distortion at the surface edges. This is why in Figure 51 the surface values for January do not follow on precisely from December.

[103] See Bill Luckin, 'Death and survival in the city: approaches to the history of disease', *Urban History Yearbook* (1980), pp. 53-62, and Bill Luckin and Graham Mooney, 'Urban history and historical epidemiology: the case of London, 1860-1920', *Urban History* 24 (1997), pp. 1-19.

Appendix 1

Registrars General of Births, Deaths and Marriages in England and Wales:
(a) Index of *Annual Reports* and *Decennial Supplements*

Report number and year to which it applies	British Parliamentary Paper reference (Cd. or Cmd. numbers also used in post-1900 catalogues)
First (1 July 1837 to 30 June 1838)	1839/XVI
Second (To year ending 30 June 1839)	1840/XVII
Third (To year ending 30 June 1840)	1841 Session 2/VI
Fourth (To year ending 30 June 1841)	1842/XIX
Fifth (1841)	1843/XXI
Sixth (1842)	1844/XIX
Seventh (1843 and 1844)	1846/XIX
Eighth (1845)	1847-1848/XXV
Ninth (1846)	1847-1848/XXV
	Appendix 1849/XXI
Tenth (1847)	1849/XXI
Eleventh (1848)	1850/XX
Twelfth (1849)	1851/XXII
Thirteenth (1850)	1852/XVII
Fourteenth (1851)	1852-1853/XL
Fifteenth (1852)	1854/XIX
Sixteenth (1853)	1854-1855/XV
Seventeenth (1854)	1856/XVIII
Eighteenth (1855)	1857 Session 2/XXII
Nineteenth (1856)	1857-1858/XXIII
Twentieth (1857)	1859/XII
Twenty-first (1858)	1860/XXIX
Twenty-second (1859)	1861/XVIII
Twenty-third (1860)	1862/XVII
Twenty-fourth (1861)	1863/XIV
Twenty-fifth (1862)	1864/XVII
Supplement for 1851-1860	Supplement 1865/XIII
Twenty-sixth (1863)	1865/XIV
Twenty-seventh (1864)	1866/XIX
Twenty-eighth (1865)	1867/XVII
Twenty-ninth (1866)	1867-1868/XIX
Thirtieth (1867)	1868-1869/XVI
Thirty-first (1868)	1870/XVI
Thirty-second (1869)	1871/XV
Thirty-third (1870)	1872/XVII
Thirty-fourth (1871)	1873/XX
Thirty-fifth (1872)	1875/XVIII, Part 1
Supplement for 1861-1870	Supplement 1875/XVIII, Part 2
Thirty-sixth (1873)	1875/XVIII, Part 1
Thirty-seventh (1874)	1876/XVIII
Thirty-eighth (1875)	1877/XXV
Thirty-ninth (1876)	1878/XXII
Fortieth (1877)	1878-1879/XIX
Forty-first (1878)	1880/XVI
Forty-second (1879)	1881/XXVII
Forty-third (1880)	1882/XIX
Forty-fourth (1881)	1883/XX
Forty-fifth (1882)	1884/XX
Supplement for 1871-1880	Supplement 1884-1885/XVII
Forty-sixth (1883)	1884-1885/XVII
Forty-seventh (1884)	1886/XVII
Forty-eighth (1885)	1886/XVII
Forty-ninth (1886)	1887/XXIII
Fiftieth (1887)	1888/XXX
Fifth-first (1888)	1889/XXV
Fifty-second (1889)	1890/XXIV
Fifty-third (1890)	1890-1891/XXIII
Fifty-fourth (1891)	1892/XXIV

Fifty-fifth (1892)	1893-1894/XXIV Part 1
Supplement for 1881-1890	Supplement 1897/XXI
Fifty-sixth (1893)	1894/XXV
Fifty-seventh (1894)	1895/XXIII Part 2
Fifty-eighth (1895)	1897/XXI
Fifty-ninth (1896)	1897/XXI
Sixtieth (1897)	1898/XVIII
Sixty-first (1898)	1899/XVI
Sixty-second (1899)	1900/XV (Cd. 323)
Sixty-third (1900)	1901/XV (Cd. 761)
Sixty-fourth (1901)	1902/XVIII (Cd. 1230)
Sixty-fifth (1902)	1904/XIV (Cd. 2003)
Supplement for 1891-1900	Supplement 1905/XVIII
	Part 1 (Cd. 2618) Part 2 (Cd. 2619)
Sixty-sixth (1903)	1904/XIV (Cd. 2197)
Sixty-seventh (1904)	1905/XVII (Cd. 2617)
Sixty-eighth (1905)	1906/XX (Cd. 3279)
Sixty-ninth (1906)	1908/XVII (Cd. 3833)
Seventieth (1907)	1909/X (Cd. 4464)
Seventy-first (1908)	1909/XI (Cd. 4961)
Seventy-second (1909)	1911/X (Cd. 5485)
Seventy-third (1910)	1911/XI (Cd. 5988)
Seventy-fourth (1911)	1912-1913/XII (Cd. 6578)
Seventy-fifth (1912)	1913/XVII (Cd. 7028)
Supplement for 1901-1910	Supplement
	Part 1 Life Tables 1914/XIV (Cd. 7512)
	Part 2 Abridged Life Tables 1920/X
	Part 3 Registration Summary Tables, 1901-
	1910 1914-1916/VIII (Cd. 8002)
Seventy-sixth (1913)	1914-1916/IX (Cd. 7780)
Seventy-seventh	1916/V (Cd. 8206)
Seventy-eighth	1917-1918/V (Cd. 8484)
Seventy-ninth	1917-1918/VI (Cd. 8869)
Eightieth	1919/X (Cmd. 40)
Eighty-first	1920/X (Cmd. 608)
Eighty-second	1920/XI (Cmd. 1017)

(b) List of Population Censuses of England and Wales from 1851

Census year	British Parliamentary Paper reference	Contents
1851	1851/XLIII	General
	1852-1853/LXXXV & LXXXVI	Comparative figures, 1801-1851
	1852-1853/LXXXVII	Place Index
	1852-1853/LXXXVIII	Age Structures and Birthplaces
1861	1861/L	General
	1862/L	Population Tables
	1863/LIII Volumes 1 & 2	Local Age Structures
1871	1871/LIX	Preliminary Report
	1872/LXVI Volumes 1 & 2	Population Tables by Counties
	1873/LXXI Volume 1	Ages
	1873/LXXI Volume 2	General Report
1881	1881/XCVI	Preliminary Report
	1883/LXXVIII	Populations for Ancient Counties
	1883/LXXIX	Registration Counties
	1883/LXXX Volumes 1 & 2	Age and Marital Condition
	1883/LXXX Volume 3	General Report
1891	1890-1891/XCIV	Preliminary Report
	1893-1894/CIV	Populations for Ancient Counties
	1893-1894/CV	Registration Counties
	1893-1894/CVI Volume 1	Age and Marital Condition
	1893-1894/CVI Volume 2	General Report
	1893-1894/CVII	Islands
	1893-1894/CIV	Index
1901	1901/XC	Preliminary Report
	1902/CXVIII to CXXI	County Reports
	1903/LXXXIV to LXXXVI	County Reports
	1903/LXXXIV Volume 1	Islands
	1903/LXXXIV Volume 2	Summary Tables
	1904/CVIII	General Report
1911	1911/LXXI	Preliminary Report
	1912-1913/CXI Volumes 1 & 2	County Reports
	1912-1913/CXII Volumes 1, 2 &3	Areas
	1912-1913/CXIII	Ages and Marital Condition
	1913/LXXVIII	Birthplace
	1913/LXXVIII & LXXIX	Occupation
	1914-1916/LXXXI	Classification of Occupations
	1917-1918/XXXV	Fertility of Marriage, Part 1
	1923 (OP.1100.20.2)	Fertility of Marriage, Part 2, Report
	1914-1916/LXXXI	Summary
	1917-1918/XXXV	General Report

Registrars General of Births, Deaths and Marriages in England and Wales: Brief notes on the contents of *Annual Reports* relevant to the *Atlas*

First Report (1 July 1837 to 30 June 1838)
Mainly on cause of death and nosology, gives age at death by single years and births (total England and Wales) and marriages (total England and Wales)

Second Report (To year ending 30 June 1839)
Has table (by counties) of proportions signing by mark, males and females separate. Gives marriages, births and deaths by divisions, also totals by counties. Also age at death and cause of death in Appendix.

Third Report (To year ending 30 June 1840)
Equivalent to Second Report

Fourth Report (To year ending 30 June 1841)
Gives marriage data by districts (also signed with a mark), also births and deaths in districts and quarters, also age at death by districts by sex and proportions signing with a mark by county, 1839-1841 (30 June year endings), plus cause of death data.

Fifth Report (1841)
Contains first life table (ELT1 for 1841, also LTs for London, Surrey and Liverpool), changes to calendar year reporting, gives marriages, births, deaths by districts for years 1839-1841 and major review of 1839-1841, also births, deaths, marriages for 1841 by districts in quarters, age at death for 1841 by districts and cause of death. Appendix by William Farr (pp. 161-178) on construction of life table, also on health of towns and public health in general.
Major analysis of mortality in London in Appendix plus map of London and Registrar's returns for separate districts.

Sixth Report (1842)
Considers illegitimacy, otherwise same pattern as Fifth Report.
Appendix of foreign returns. Annuity calculations on ELT1, pp. 290-358.

Seventh Report (1843 and 1844)
Same pattern as Fifth and Sixth Reports. Major Statistical Nosology. LT for Manchester, 1841. Appendix gives sample of census schedule 1801- for Kent example.

Eight Report (1845)
Same pattern as Fifth, Sixth, and Seventh Reports.
Report gives births/women 15-45, gives illegitimate births data and age-structure of enumerated population in 1841 by districts of London, gives births totals for 1839-1844 (by years) and age at death 1838-1844 (by years) for districts.

Farr writes on Northampton LT, pp. 290-325.

Ninth Report (1846)
Same layout as Fifth to Eighth Reports with no special items.
Appendix to Ninth Report in 3 parts:
Part 1 reviews mortality rates 1838-1844 by districts,
Part 2 on population totals by districts 1801-1841 census,
Part 3 on age structure data by districts for 1841 (also has index of districts, and sub-districts).

Tenth Report (1847)
Very short, only uses counties, nothing on cause or age at death, but gives births, marriages and deaths by quarters for the year.

Eleventh Report (1848)
As for Tenth.

Twelfth Report (1849)
As for Tenth

Thirteenth Report (1850)
As for Tenth.

Fourteenth Report (1851)
As for Tenth.

Fifteenth Report (1852)
As for Tenth.

Sixteenth Report (1953)
As for Tenth. Gives revised Statistical Nosology.

Seventeenth Report (1854)
As for Tenth.

Eighteenth Report (1855)
New format with a full report on marriages (with mark), births, deaths, cause of death, age at death by registration districts, gives births by sub-districts too.

Nineteenth Report (1856)
As Eighteenth, plus special tables on violent death. Letter from Farr on causes of death. Index of districts, pp. 223-6.

Twentieth Report (1857)
As Eighteenth. Letter from Farr on causes of death related to economic data. ELT2 for women.

Twenty-first Report (1858)
As for Twentieth, with Farr letter.

Twenty-second Report (1859)
As for Twenty-first with Farr causes of death letter.

Twenty-third Report (1860)
As for Twenty-first. Has marriages, births and deaths for 1851-1860 by districts and births and deaths for sub-districts, but just totals of marriages, births and deaths. Farr letter on causes of death.

Twenty-fourth Report (1861)
As for Twenty-first. Deaths in public institutions in London and other districts. Farr letter on causes of death.

Twenty-fifth Report (1862)
As for Twenty-third. Farr letter on causes of death. Index to districts and sub-districts.
Supplement to Twenty-fifth Report (1851-1860)
Analysis by Farr of causes of death for 1851-1860 with causes of death, for ages by districts. Gives deaths in occupations for 1860-1861. Population density by districts related to average mortality for 1841-1850 and 1851-1860.
Major statistical set.

Twenty-sixth Report (1863)
As for Twenty-fifth. Farr on causes of death.

Twenty-seventy Report (1864)
As for Twenty-fifth. Farr on causes plus some extra tables. Gives mid-year estimates for 1801-1866 in Report.

Twenty-eighth Report (1865)
As for Twenty-seventh. Farr on causes of death. Report has details on emigration also mid-year estimates and ELT3 for 1838-1854. (Relates to *English Life Table. With an Introduction by W. Farr* (London: Longmans, 1864).)

Twenty-ninth Report (1866)
As with Twenty-eighth Report, has emigration and mid-year estimates also Farr on causes of death.

Thirtieth Report (1867)
As for Twenty-ninth, all aspects.

Thirty-first Report (1868)
As for Thirtieth, all aspects.

Thirty-second Report (1869)
As for Thirtieth, has deaths in large public institutions by districts.

Thirty-third Report (1870)
As for Thirtieth, has births, marriages and deaths for 1861-1870 plus Farr's cause of death letter, also has LTs for Healthy Districts.

Thirty-fourth Report (1871)
As for Thirtieth. Special report on infant mortality linked with Farr's letter.

Thirty-fifth Report (1872)
As for Thirtieth.
Supplement to Thirty-fifth Report (1861-1870)
Introduced by Farr, has pattern similar to previous Supplement to Twenty-fifth Report.

Thirty-sixth Report (1873)
As for Thirtieth.

Thirty-seventh Report (1874)
As for Thirtieth.

Thirty-eighth Report (1875)
As for Thirtieth. Farr's letter contains some long-term (1848-1875) cause of death figures.

Thirty-ninth Report (1876)
As for Thirty-eighth.

Fortieth Report (1877)
As for Thirty-eighth. Farr develops mortality/population density 'law' outlined in Fifth Report.

Forty-first Report (1878)
As for Thirty-eighth. Farr's letter is very short.

Forty-second Report (1879)
As for Thirty-eighth. No letter from Farr.

Forty-Third Report (1880)
As for Forty-second. (Ogle's first Report.)

Forty-fourth Report (1881)
As for Forty-third, but only gives age at death by districts for total population, not men and women separately. Revised nosology.

Forty-fifth Report (1882)
As for Forty-fourth.
Supplement to Forty-fifth Report (1871-1880)
Usual format for *Decennial Supplement*: age at death, by cause for districts, also occupational mortality data.

Forty-sixth Report (1883)
As for Forty-fourth.

Forty-seventh Report (1884)
As for Forty-fourth.

Forty-eighth Report (1885)
As for Forty-fourth, but only gives age at death for counties for men and women.

Forty-Ninth Report (1886)
As for Forty-eighth.

Fiftieth Report (1887)
As for Forty-eighth, but with special note on fifty years of civil registration.

Fifty-first Report (1888)
As for Forty-eighth.

Fifty-second Report (1889)
As for Forty-eighth.

Fifty-third Report (1890)
As for Forty-eighth.

Fifty-fourth Report (1891)
As for Forty-eighth.

Fifty-fifth Report (1892)
As for Forty-eighth
Supplement to Fifty-fifth Report (1881-1890)
Part 1. Introduction by John Tatham contains new ELT for 1881-1890 has a density of population to death rate analysis for districts, 1841-1850, 1851-1860, 1861-180, 1871-1880, 1881-1890.

Very similar to other *Decennial Supplements,* has age at death by cause for districts tables.
Part 2. Mainly on occupational mortality, 1890-1892, by cause and age at death.

Fifty-sixth Report (1893)
As for Forty-eighth.

Fifty-seventh Report (1894)
As for Forty-eighth.

Fifty-eighth Report (1895)
As for Forth-eighth.

Fifty-ninth Report (1896)
As for Forty-eighth, but Report more elaborate than usual e.g. relation between marriage rate and commercial activity. Revised nosology.

Sixtieth Report (1897)
As for Forty-eighth.

Sixty-first Report (1898)
As for Forty-eighth.

Sixty-second Report (1899)
As for Forty-eighth.

Sixty-third Report (1900)
As for Forty-eighth.

Sixty-fourth Report (1901)
As for Forty-eighth.

Sixty-fifth Report (1902)
As for Forty-eighth.
Supplement to Sixty-fifth Report (1891-1900)
Part 1. Conventional Supplement: causes by age by districts etc., also has life table data.
Part 2. On occupational mortality for 1900-1903.

Sixty-sixth Report (1903)
As for Forty-eighth.

Sixty-seventh Report (1904)
As for Forty-eighth. Letter on causes of death from John Tatham.

Sixty-eighth Report (1905)
As for Sixty-seventh, but with tables on legitimate birth rates and survivors by counties in Report, Tables B and C.

Sixty-ninth Report (1906)
As for Sixty-seventh.

Seventieth Report (1907)
As for Sixty-seventh.

Seventy-first Report (1908)
As for Sixty-seventh. T. H. C. Stevenson takes over writing letter on causes of death to new Registrar General, Bernard Mallet.

Seventy-second Report (1909)
As for Sixty-seventh. Graphs in report on birth rate. Start of *Statistical Review of the Year* by T. H. C. Stevenson.

Seventy-third Report (1910)
As for Seventy-second with Stevenson's *Review*

Seventy-fourth Report (1911)
New style with local government areas, but retains Stevenson's *Review.*

Seventy-fifth Report (1912)
As for Seventy-fourth. Gives some data on occupations and fertility in Stevenson's *Review.*
Supplement to Seventy-fifth Report (1901-1910)
Part 1. Life Tables by George King. Gives details for ELT7 for 1901-1910 and ELT8 for 1910-1912.
Part 2. Abridged Life Tables by E. C. Snow. Gives County and County Borough life tables of 1911-1912, males and females separately.
Part 3. Registration summary tables, 1901-1910. Mainly cause of death by age by district but also review of the *Vital Statistics of England and Wales during the Period of Ten Years, 1901-10* by T. H. C. Stevenson.

Seventy-sixth Report (1913)
As for Seventy-fourth.

Bibliography

Anderson, Michael, 'The social implications of demographic change', in F. M. L. Thompson (ed.), *The Cambridge Social History of Britain, 1750-1950, Volume 2, People and their Environment* (Cambridge: Cambridge University Press, 1990), pp. 1-70

Anderson, Olive, *Suicide in Victorian and Edwardian England* (Oxford: Clarendon Press, 1987)

Anderson, Roy M. and Robert M. May, *Infectious Diseases of Humans: Dynamics and Control* (Oxford: Oxford University Press, 1992)

Barker, David J. P., 'Rise and fall of Western diseases', *Nature* 338 (1989), pp. 371-372

Barker, David J. P., *Mothers, Babies, and Diseases in Later Life* (London: BMJ Publishing Group, 1994)

Britton, M. (ed.), *Mortality and Geography: A Review of the Mid-1980s*, Registrar General's Decennial Supplement for England and Wales, Series DS No. 9 (London: HMSO, 1990)

Brownlee, John, *An Investigation into the Epidemiology of Phthisis in Great Britain and Ireland, Parts I, II and III*, Medical Research Council, Special Reports Nos. 18 and 46 (London: HMSO, 1918 and 1922)

Brownlee, John, 'Periodicities of epidemics of measles in the large towns of Great Britain and Ireland', *Proceedings of the Royal Society of Medicine* (Epidemiology Section) 12 (1-2) (1919), pp. 77-120

Brownlee, John, 'Density and death-rate: Farr's law', *Journal of the Royal Statistical Society* 83 (1920), pp. 280-283

Bryder, Linda, *Below the Magic Mountain: A Social History of Tuberculosis in the Twentieth Century* (Oxford: Clarendon Press, 1988)

Bryder, Linda, ''Not always one and the same thing': the registration of tuberculosis deaths in Britain, 1900-1950', *Social History of Medicine* 9 (1996), pp. 253-265

Bull, Thomas, *The Maternal Management of Children in Health and Disease* (London: Longman, Green, Longman, and Robert, seventh edition 1861)

Bynum, W. F., *Science and the Practice of Medicine in the Nineteenth Century* (Cambridge: Cambridge University Press, 1994)

Champion, Tony *et al.*, *The Population of Britain in the 1990s: A Social and Economic Atlas* (Oxford: Clarendon Press, 1996)

Cliff, Andrew D. and Peter Haggett, *Atlas of Disease Distributions: Analytic Approaches to Epidemiological Data* (Oxford: Blackwell, 1988)

Cliff, Andrew D., Peter Haggett and Matthew Smallman-Raynor, *Measles: An Historical Geography of a Major Human Viral Disease from Global Expansion to Local Retreat, 1840-1980* (Oxford: Blackwell, 1993)

Coale, Ansley J. and Susan Cotts Watkins (eds.), *The Decline of Fertility in Europe* (Princeton: Princeton University Press, 1986)

Creighton, Charles, *A History of Epidemics in Britain, Volume Two, From the Extinction of the Plague to the Present Time* (Cambridge: Cambridge University Press, 1894)

Cronjé, Gillian, 'Tuberculosis and mortality decline in England and Wales, 1851-1910', in Robert Woods and John Woodward (eds.), *Urban Disease and Mortality in Nineteenth-Century England* (London: Batsford, 1984), pp. 79-101

Dorling, Daniel, *A New Social Atlas of Britain* (Chichester: Wiley, 1995)

Durkheim, Emile, *Le Suicide. Etude de Sociologie* (Paris: Félix Alcan, 1897)

Eyler, John M., 'Mortality statistics and Victorian health policy: program and criticism', *Bulletin of the History of Medicine* 50 (1976), pp. 335-355

Eyler, John M., *Victorian Social Medicine: The Ideas and Methods of William Farr* (Baltimore: Johns Hopkins University Press, 1979)

Eyler, John M., 'The conceptual origins of William Farr's epidemiology: numerical methods and social thought in the 1830s', in Abraham M. Lilienfeld (ed.), *Times, Places, and Persons: Aspects of the History of Epidemiology* (Baltimore: Johns Hopkins University Press, 1980), pp. 1-21

Eyler, John M., 'Scarlet fever and confinement: the Edwardian debate over isolation hospitals', *Bulletin of the History of Medicine* 61 (1987), pp. 1-24

Farr, William, 'On the construction of life-tables; illustrated by a new life-table of the healthy districts of England', *Philosophical Transactions of the Royal Society of London* 149 (1859), pp. 837-878

Farr, William, *English Life Table. Tables of Lifetimes, Annuities, and Premiums* (London: Longmans, Green and Co., 1864)

Farr, William, *Vital Statistics* (London: Sanitary Institute of Great Britain, edited by Noel Humphreys, 1885)

Floud, Roderick, Kenneth Wachter and Annabel Gregory, *Height, Health and History: Nutritional Status in the United Kingdom, 1750-1980* (Cambridge: Cambridge University Press, 1990)

Fogel, Robert W., 'Economic growth, population theory, and physiology: the bearing of long-term processes on the making of economic policy', *American Economic Review* 84 (1994), pp. 369-395

Fogel, Robert W., 'The relevance of Malthus for the study of mortality today: long-run influences on health, mortality, labour force participation, and population growth', in Kerstin Lindahl-Kiessling and Hans Landberg (eds.), *Population, Economic Development and the Environment* (Oxford: Oxford University Press, 1994), pp. 231-284

Fridlizius, Gunnar, 'The deformation of cohorts: nineteenth-century mortality decline in a generational perspective', *Scandinavian Economic History Review* 37 (1989), pp. 3-17

Galley, Chris, Naomi Williams and Robert Woods, 'Detection without correction: problems in assessing the quality of English ecclesiastical and civil registration', *Annales de Démographie Historique* (1995), pp. 161-183.

Gardner, M. J., P. D. Winter and David J. P. Barker, *Atlas of Mortality from Selected Diseases in England and Wales, 1968-1978* (Chichester: Wiley, 1984)

Glass, D. V., 'A note on the under-registration of births in Britain in the nineteenth century', *Population Studies* 5 (1951), pp. 70-88

Guha, Sumit, 'The importance of social intervention in England's mortality decline: the evidence reviewed', *Social History of Medicine* 7 (1994), pp. 89-113

Hardy, Anne, *The Epidemic Streets: Infectious Disease and the Rise of Preventive Medicine, 1856-1900* (Oxford: Clarendon Press, 1993)

Hardy, Anne, ''Death is the cure of all diseases': using the General Register Office cause of death statistics for 1837-1920', *Social History of Medicine* 7 (1994), pp. 472-492

Higgs, Edward, 'A cuckoo in the nest? The origins of civil registration and state medical statistics in England and Wales', *Continuity and Change* 11 (1996), pp. 115-134

Higgs, Edward, 'The statistical Big Bang of 1911: ideology, technological innovation and the production of medical statistics', *Social History of Medicine* 9 (1996), pp. 409-426

Howe, G. Melvyn, *National Atlas of Disease Mortality in the United Kingdom* (London: Thomas Nelson and Sons, 1963, second edition 1970)

Howe, G. Melvyn, *Man, Environment and Diseases in Britain* (Newton Abbot: David & Charles, 1972)

Humphries, Jane, ''Bread and a pennyworth of treacle': excess female mortality in England in the 1840s', *Cambridge Journal of Economics* 15 (1991), pp. 451-473

Illsley, Raymond and Julian Le Grand, 'Regional inequalities in mortality', *Journal of Epidemiology and Community Health* 47 (1993), pp. 444-449

Jalland, Pat, *Death in the Victorian Family* (Oxford: Oxford University Press, 1996)

Johansson, S. Ryan, 'Rhetoric and reality in modern mortality history', *Historical Methods* 27 (1994), pp. 101-125

Jones, Hugh R., 'The perils and protection of infant life', *Journal of the Royal Statistical Society* 57 (1894), pp. 1-98

Kayne, George Gregory, Water Pagel and Laurence O'Shaughnessy, *Pulmonary Tuberculosis: Pathology, Diagnosis, Management and Prevention* (Oxford: Oxford University Press, 1939)

Kearns, Gerry, 'Zvilis and Hygaeia: urban public health and the epidemiologic transition', in Richard Lawton (ed.), *The Rise and Fall of Great Cities* (London: Belhaven Press, 1989), pp. 100-120

Kearns, Gerry, 'Le handicap urbaine et le décline de la mortalité en Angleterre et du Pays de Galles, 1851-1911', *Annales de Démographie Historique* (1993), pp. 75-105

Kearns, Gerry and C. W. J. Withers (eds.), *Urbanizing Britain* (Cambridge: Cambridge University Press, 1991)

King, George and Arthur Newsholme, 'On the alleged increase of cancer', *Journal of the Institute of Actuaries* 36 (1893), pp. 120-150

Kintner, Hallie J., 'Classifying causes of death during the late nineteenth and early twentieth centuries: the case of German infant mortality', *Historical Methods* 19 (1986), pp. 45-54

Kiple, Kenneth (ed.), *The Cambridge World History of Human Disease* (Cambridge: Cambridge University Press, 1993)

Koch, Robert, 'How the fight against tuberculosis now stands', *Lancet* 1 (4317) (1906), pp. 1449-1451

Laing, James S, 'Whooping cough: its prevalence and mortality in Aberdeen', *Public Health* 14 (10) (1902), pp. 584-599

Law, C. M., 'The growth of urban population in England and Wales, 1801-1911', *Transactions of the Institute of British Geographers* 41 (1967), pp. 125-143

Lawton, Richard, 'Population changes in England and Wales in the later nineteenth century: an analysis of trends by registration districts', *Transactions of the Institute of British Geographers* 44 (1968), pp. 55-74

Lawton, Richard, 'Urbanisation and population change in nineteenth-century England', in John Patten (ed.), *The Expanding City* (London: Academic Press, 1983), pp. 179-224

Laxton, Paul and Naomi Williams, 'Urbanization and infant mortality in England: a long term perspective and review', in Marie C. Nelson and John Rogers (eds.), *Urbanisation and the Epidemiologic Transition*, Reports from the Family History Group, Department of History, Uppsala University, No. 9 (Uppsala, 1989), pp. 109-135

Lee, R. D. and D. Lam, 'Age distribution adjustments for English censuses, 1821 to 1931', *Population Studies* 37 (1983), pp. 445-464

Logan, W. P. D., 'Mortality in England and Wales from 1848 to 1947. A survey of the changing causes of death during the past hundred years', *Population Studies* 5 (1950), pp. 132-178

Loudon, Irvine, *Death in Childbirth: An International Study of Maternal Care and Maternal Mortality, 1800-1950* (Oxford: Clarendon Press, 1992)

Louis, Pierre-Charles-Alexandre, 'Note sur la fréquence relative de la phthisie chez les deux sexes', *Annales d'Hygiène Publique* 6 (1831), pp. 49-57

Luckin, Bill, 'Death and survival in the city: approaches to the history of disease', *Urban History Yearbook* (1980), pp. 53-62

Luckin, Bill and Graham Mooney, 'Urban history and historical epidemiology: the case of London, 1860-1920', *Urban History* 24 (1997), pp. 1-19.

McKeown, Thomas, *The Modern Rise of Population* (London: Edward Arnold, 1976)

McKeown, Thomas and C. R. Lowe, *An Introduction to Social Medicine* (Oxford: Blackwell, 1966)

McKeown, Thomas and R. G. Record, 'Reasons for the decline of mortality in England and Wales during the nineteenth century', *Population Studies* 16 (1962), pp. 94-122

McKeown, Thomas, R. G. Record and R. D. Turner, 'An interpretation of the decline of mortality in England and Wales during the twentieth century', *Population Studies* 29 (1975), pp. 391-422

Mercer, A. J., *Disease, Mortality and Population in Transition: Epidemioogical-Demographic Change as Part of a Global Phenomenon* (Leicester: Leicester University Press, 1990)

Mooney, Graham, 'Did London pass the 'sanitary test'? Seasonal infant mortality in London, 1870-1914', *Journal of Historical Geography* 20 (1994), pp. 158-174

Mooney, Graham, 'Still-births and the measurement of urban infant mortality rates c. 1890-1930', *Local Population Studies* 53 (1994), pp. 42-52

Mooney, Graham, *The Geography of Mortality Decline in Victorian London* (Unpublished PhD Thesis, University of Liverpool, 1994)

Munro, A. Campbell, 'Measles: an epidemiological study', *Transactions of the Epidemiological Society* 10 (1890-1891), pp. 94-109

Nelson, Marie C., 'Diphtheria in late-nineteenth-century Sweden: policy and practice', *Continuity and Change* 9 (1994), pp. 213-224

Newsholme, Arthur, *The Elements of Vital Statistics in their Bearing on Social and Public Health Problems* (London: George Allen and Unwin, first edition 1889, third edition 1923)

Newsholme, Arthur, 'The vital statistics of Peabody Buildings and other artisans' and labourers' block dwellings', *Journal of the Royal Statistical Society* 54 (1891), pp. 70-97

Newsholme, Arthur, *Epidemic Diphtheria: A Research on the Origin and Spread of the Disease from an International Standpoint* (London: Swan Sonnenschein, 1898)

Newsholme, Arthur, 'A contribution to the study of epidemic diarrhoea', *Public Health* 12 (3) (1899), pp. 139-210

Newsholme, Arthur, 'The statistics of cancer', *The Practitioner* (April 1899), pp. 371-384

Newsholme, Arthur, 'The utility of isolation hospitals in diminishing the spread of scarlet fever', *Journal of Hygiene* 1 (1901), pp. 145-152

Newsholme, Arthur, 'An inquiry into the principal causes of the reduction in the death-rate from phthisis during the last forty years, with special reference to the segregation of phthisical patients in general institutions', *Journal of Hygiene* 6 (1906), pp. 304-384

Newsholme, Arthur, 'The measurement of progress in public health with special reference to the life and work of William Farr', *Economica* 9 (1923), pp. 186-202

Nissel, Muriel, *People Count: A History of the General Register Office* (London: HMSO, 1987)

Ogle, William, 'Suicides in England and Wales in relation to age, sex, season and occupation', *Journal of the Statistical Society* 49 (1886), pp. 101-135

Payne, Henry, *A Pocket Vocabulary of Medical Terms (with their pronunciation), for the use of Registrars, Poor Law Officials, &C.* (London: Hadden, Best & Co, 1885)

Porter, Roy (ed.), *Cambridge Illustrated History of Medicine* (Cambridge: Cambridge University Press, 1996)

Preston, Samuel H., *Mortality Patterns in National Populations* (New York: Academic Press, 1976)

Preston, Samuel H. and Michael R. Haines, *Fatal Years: Child Mortality in Late Nineteenth-Century America* (Princeton: Princeton University Press, 1991)

Preston, Samuel, Nathan Keyfitz and Robert Schoen, *Causes of Death: Life Tables for National Populations* (New York: Seminar Press, 1972)

Radcliffe, John Netten, 'On the distribution of suicides in England and Wales', *Journal of Psychological Medicine* 11 (1859), pp. 582-602

Ransome, Arthur, 'On the form of the epidemic wave, and some of its probable causes', *Transactions of the Epidemiological Society* 1 (1881-1882), pp. 96-107

Riley, James C., 'Excess mortality in youth', in David S. Reher and Roger Schofield (eds.), *Old and New Methods in Historical Demography* (Oxford: Clarendon Press, 1993), pp. 394-409

Riley, James C., *Sick, Not Dead: The Health of British Workingmen during the Mortality Decline* (Baltimore: Johns Hopkins University Press, 1997)

Schofield, R. S., 'Did the mothers really die? Three centuries of maternal mortality in 'The World We Have Lost'', in L. Bonfield, R. M. Smith and K. Wrightson (eds.), *The World We Have Gained: Histories of Population and Social Structure* (Oxford: Blackwell, 1986), pp. 231-260

Sloggett, Andrew and Heather Joshi, 'Higher mortality in deprived areas: community or personal disadvantages?', *British Medical Journal* 309 (1994), pp. 1470-1474

Smith, F. B., *The People's Health, 1830-1910* (London: Croom Helm, 1979)

Smith, F. B., *The Retreat of Tuberculosis, 1850-1950* (London: Croom Helm, 1988)

Sullivan, Jeremiah M., Shea Oscar Rutstein and George T. Bicego, *Infant and Child Mortality, Demographic and Health Surveys Comparative Studies No. 15* (Calverton, Maryland: Macro International Inc., 1994)

Sutherland, Ian, 'Recent studies in the epidemiology of tuberculosis', *Advances in Tuberculosis Research* 19 (1976), pp. 1-63

Szreter, Simon, 'The importance of social intervention in Britain's mortality decline *c* 1850-1914: a re-interpretation of the role of public health', *Social History of Medicine* 1 (1988), pp. 1-37

Szreter, Simon (ed.), *The General Register Office of England and Wales and the Public Health Movement, 1837-1914, A Comparative Perspective, Social History of Medicine*, Special Issue, 4 (3) (1991), pp. 401-537

Szreter, Simon, 'Mortality in England in the eighteenth and nineteenth centuries: a reply to Sumit Guha', *Social History of Medicine* 7 (1994), pp. 269-282

Tabutin, Dominique 'La surmortalité féminine en Europe avant 1940', *Population* 33 (1) (1978), pp. 121-148

Teitelbaum, Michael S., 'Birth underregistration in the constituent counties of England and Wales: 1841-1910', *Population Studies* 28 (1974), pp. 329-343.

Teitelbaum, Michael S., *The British Fertility Decline: Demographic Transition in the Crucible of the Industrial Revolution* (Princeton: Princeton University Press, 1984)

Vallin, Jacques, 'Mortality in Europe from 1720 to 1914: long-term trends and changes in patterns by age and sex', in Roger Schofield, David Reher and Alain Bideau (eds.), *The Decline of Mortality in Europe* (Oxford: Clarendon Press, 1991), pp. 38-67

Welton, T. A., 'The effects of migration in disturbing local rates of mortality as exemplified in the statistics of London and the surrounding country for the years 1851-60', *Journal of the Institute of Actuaries* 16 (1872), pp. 153-186

West, Charles, *Lectures on the Diseases of Infancy and Childhood* (London: Longmans, Green and Co., seventh edition 1884)

Whitelegge, B. Arthur, 'Measles epidemics, major and minor', *Transactions of the Epidemiological Society* 12 (1892-1893), pp. 37-54

Williams, Naomi, 'Death in its season: class, environment and the mortality of children in nineteenth-century Sheffield', *Social History of Medicine* 5 (1992), pp. 71-94

Williams, Naomi, 'The implementation of compulsory health legislation: infant smallpox vaccination in England and Wales, 1840-1890', *Journal of Historical Geography* 20 (1994), pp. 396-412

Williams, Naomi, 'The reporting and classification of causes of death in mid-nineteenth-century England: the example of Sheffield', *Historical Methods* 29 (1996), pp. 58-71

Williams, Naomi and Chris Galley, 'Urban-rural differentials in infant mortality in Victorian England', *Population Studies* 49 (1995), pp. 401-420

Williams, Naomi and Graham Mooney, 'Infant mortality in an 'Age of Great Cities': London and the English provincial cities compared, c. 1840-1910', *Continuity and Change* 9 (1994), pp. 185-212

Williamson, Jeffrey G., *Coping with City Growth During the British Industrial Revolution* (Cambridge: Cambridge University Press, 1990)

Wilson, Chris and Robert Woods, 'Fertility in England: a long-term perspective', *Population Studies* 45 (1991), pp. 399-415

Wilson, George N., 'Measles: its prevalence and mortality in Aberdeen', *Public Health* 18 (2) (1905), pp. 65-82

Wilson, Leonard G., 'The historical decline of tuberculosis in Europe and America: its causes and significance', *Journal of the History of Medicine* 45 (1990), pp. 49-57

Wohl, Anthony S., *Endangered Lives: Public Health in Victorian Britain* (London: Dent, 1983)

Woods, Robert, 'Mortality and sanitary conditions in late-nineteenth-century Birmingham', in Robert Woods and John Woodward (eds.), *Urban Disease and Mortality in Nineteenth-Century England* (London: Batsford, 1984), pp. 176-202

Woods, Robert, 'The effects of population redistribution on the level of mortality in nineteenth-century England and Wales', *Journal of Economic History* 45 (1985), pp. 645-651

Woods, R. I., 'Approaches to the fertility transition in Victorian England', *Population Studies* 41 (1987), pp. 283-311

Woods, Robert, 'Public health and public hygiene: the urban environment in the late nineteenth and early twentieth centuries', in Roger Schofield, David Reher and Alain Bideau (eds.), *The Decline of Mortality in Europe* (Oxford: Clarendon Press, 1991), pp. 233-247

Woods, Robert, 'On the historical relationship between infant and adult mortality', *Population Studies* 47 (1993), pp. 195-219

Woods, Robert, *The Population of Britain in the Nineteenth Century* (Cambridge: Cambridge University Press, 1995)

Woods, Robert, 'Physician, heal thyself: the health and mortality of Victorian doctors', *Social History of Medicine* 9 (1996), pp. 1-30, also 10 (1997), pp. 157-163

Woods, Robert and P. R. Andrew Hinde, 'Mortality in Victorian England: models and patterns', *Journal of Interdisciplinary History* 18 (1987), pp. 27-54

Woods, R. I., P. A. Watterson and J. H. Woodward, 'The causes of rapid infant mortality decline in England and Wales, 1861-1921. Parts I and II', *Population Studies* 42 (1988), pp. 343-366 and 43 (1989), pp. 113-132

Woods, Robert and John Woodward (eds.), *Urban Disease and Mortality in Nineteenth-Century England* (London: Batsford, 1984)

Woods, Robert and Naomi Williams, 'Must the gap widen before it can be narrowed? Long-term trends in social class mortality differentials', *Continuity and Change* 10 (1995), pp. 105-137

Woods, Robert, Naomi Williams and Chris Galley, 'Differential mortality patterns among infants and other young children: the experience of England and Wales in the nineteenth century', in Carlo A Corsini and Pier Paolo Viazzo (eds.), *The Decline of Infant and Child Mortality: The European Experience, 1750-1990* (The Hague: Kluwer, 1997), pp. 57-72

Wrigley, E. A., 'Births and baptisms: the use of Anglican baptism registers as a source of information about the numbers of births in England before the beginning of civil registration', *Population Studies* 31 (1977), pp. 281-312

Wrigley, E. A., *People, Cities and Wealth* (Oxford: Blackwell, 1987)

Wrigley, E. A. and R. S. Schofield, *The Population History of England, 1541-1871: A Reconstruction* (London: Edward Arnold, 1981; Cambridge: Cambridge University Press, 1989)

Wrigley, E. A. *et al.*, *The Population History of England from Family Reconstitutions* (Cambridge: Cambridge University Press, 1997)

Young, Matthew, 'An investigation into the periodicity of epidemics of whooping-cough from 1870-1910 by means of the periodogram', *Proceedings of the Royal Society of Medicine* (Epidemiology Section) 13 (1-2) (1920), pp. 207-236

Index

Map A. Location map for selected districts of England and Wales

Newcastle upon Tyne
Sunderland
Middlesborough
Bradford
York
Leeds
Hull
Sheffield
Derby
Nottingham
Leicester

Carlisle
Blackburn
Preston
Manchester
Liverpool
Stoke on Trent

Wolverhampton
Birmingham
Coventry
Gloucester

Norwich
Cambridge
Bury St Edmunds
Ipswich
Colchester
West Ham
Canterbury
Dover

Swansea
Cardiff
Bristol
Exeter
Plymouth
Penzance

Oxford
Reading
Portsmouth
Southampton
Brighton
Eastbourne

0   50   100 km

Map B. Location map for the registration counties of England and Wales

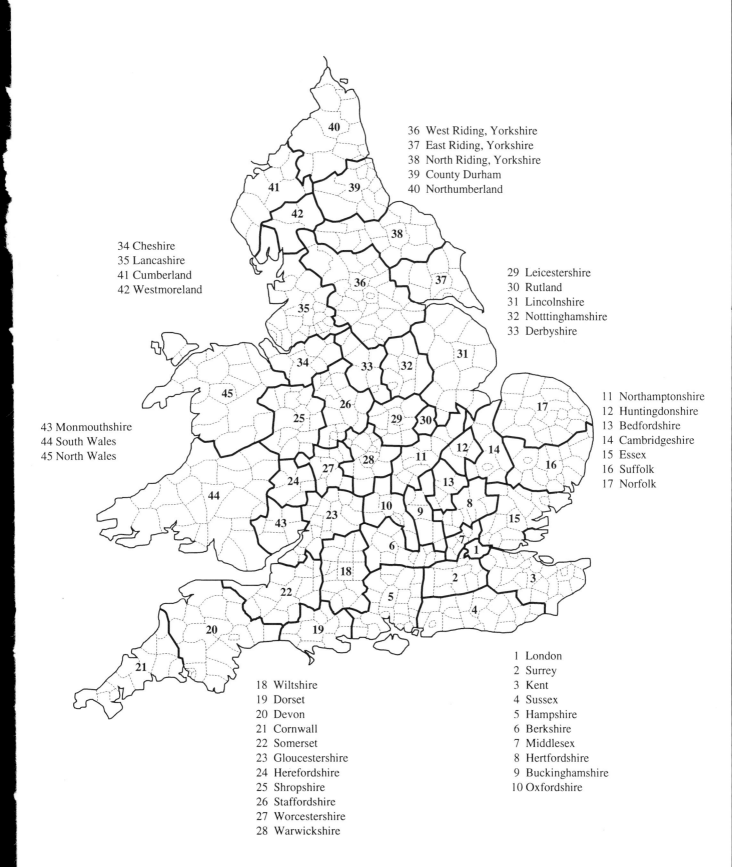

36 West Riding, Yorkshire
37 East Riding, Yorkshire
38 North Riding, Yorkshire
39 County Durham
40 Northumberland

34 Cheshire
35 Lancashire
41 Cumberland
42 Westmoreland

29 Leicestershire
30 Rutland
31 Lincolnshire
32 Notttinghamshire
33 Derbyshire

43 Monmouthshire
44 South Wales
45 North Wales

11 Northamptonshire
12 Huntingdonshire
13 Bedfordshire
14 Cambridgeshire
15 Essex
16 Suffolk
17 Norfolk

18 Wiltshire
19 Dorset
20 Devon
21 Cornwall
22 Somerset
23 Gloucestershire
24 Herefordshire
25 Shropshire
26 Staffordshire
27 Worcestershire
28 Warwickshire

1 London
2 Surrey
3 Kent
4 Sussex
5 Hampshire
6 Berkshire
7 Middlesex
8 Hertfordshire
9 Buckinghamshire
10 Oxfordshire

Map C. Location map for the districts of London

1 Kensington, Paddington, Fulham
2 Chelsea
3 St George Hanover Sq
4 Westminister, St James Westminster
5 Marylebone
6 Hampstead
7 St Pancras
8 Islington
9 Hackney

10 St Giles
11 Strand, St Martin in the Fields
12 Holborn, Clerkenwell, St Luke
13 City of London, East London, West London
14 Shoreditch
15 Bethnal Green
16 Whitechapel
17 St George in the East
18 Stepney, Mile End Old Town
19 Poplar

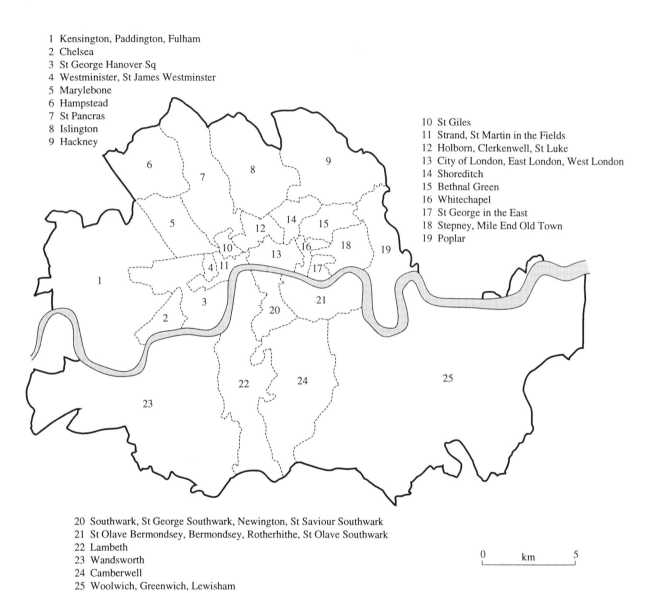

20 Southwark, St George Southwark, Newington, St Saviour Southwark
21 St Olave Bermondsey, Bermondsey, Rotherhithe, St Olave Southwark
22 Lambeth
23 Wandsworth
24 Camberwell
25 Woolwich, Greenwich, Lewisham

0   km   5